"In your hands is an excellent book on new and emerging forms of missional church and discipleship by an outstanding practitioner of the ideas proposed in it. These are hard won insights from the frontline of the church in North America. All hail, Caesar!"

—**ALAN HIRSCH**, Founder of Forge Mission Training network,
Future Travelers, and award-winning author on
missional Christianity in Western contexts.
www.alanhirsch.org

"The world sets a high measure for big thinking and speedy growth. In *Small is Big, Slow is Fast,* Caeser Kalinowski challenges us to redefine success and live under a different paradigm— one where kings are born in mangers and the smallest deeds can multiply results beyond our imagination. It will challenge you and motive you toward mission."

—**ED STETZER**, www.edstetzer.com

Small is Big, Slow is Fast is an interesting read and more! Caesar Kalinowski has authored a book about how to live, walk, and lead like Jesus in today's culture. This book will encourage you to live the life we were meant to live as followers of Jesus by loving people, creating community, and along the way changing the world.

—**DAVE FERGUSON**, Lead Pastor,
Community Christian Church, Illinois

SMALL IS BIG
SLOW IS FAST

CAESAR KALINOWSKI

SMALL IS BIG
SLOW IS FAST

Living and Leading Your Family
and Community on God's Mission

ZONDERVAN

Small Is Big, Slow Is Fast
Copyright © 2014 by Caesar Kalinowski

This title is also available as a Zondervan ebook.
Visit www.zondervan.com/ebooks.

Requests for information should be addressed to:

Zondervan, 3900 *Sparks Drive SE, Grand Rapids, Michigan 49546*

ISBN 978-0-310-51701-6

Published in association with the literary agency of WordServe Literary Group, Ltd., Highland Ranch, Colorado 80130. (www.wordserveliterary.com)

Cover design: Studio Gearbox
Cover photos: © amwu/www.istock.com, © GlobalP/www.istock.com
Interior design: Greg Johnson/Textbook Perfect

Printed in the United States of America

HB 09.21.2017

*This book and the work that went into it comes from my heart
and is for all of those longing to be disciples who live in the ways of
Jesus — here, now, today — and lead others to do the same.
To God be the glory!*

CONTENTS

FOREWORD

by Hugh Halter

After twenty-five years of pastoral ministry, I now realize that most of my methods, metrics, and personal vision for life and influence with people didn't work out the way I thought they would. If you've committed your life to serving Jesus, my guess is that you've come to similar conclusions. Your vision and mission statements didn't move people, your programs didn't change the world, and your preaching didn't bring in the masses. The reality of life and leadership in Christ's church can leave you a tad jaded and despondent, wondering if anything works.

Well, the way of Jesus does work! And the idea that small is big, slow is fast is a welcome reminder of critical nuances that most people miss.

I met Caesar during my ministry journey, and I have found him to be a brash reality, a fresh voice, an encouraging coach, and a faithful friend. I've also spent many hours in Caesar and Tina's home in both Tacoma and now New York City, and the consistency of their life into the lost world is a beacon of hope. Caesar's life is valid proof that he has tapped into some secrets Jesus hoped to reveal to us all.

As you read, I believe you will find yourself saying, "Why didn't I see that? Why do I keep doing this? He makes it sound so doable. This is what I will now give my life to." But Caesar is too wise to tell you exactly what you should do and how to do it. Instead, you will see in his stories and concepts a biblical plumb line to keep your journey true, your heart clean, and your influence sure.

Thank you, Caesar, for not taking the easy route or relying on your reputation to pave a smooth road. You've lived in the trenches of humanity as a light to both onlookers and leaders, and I pray that your life's work to date will be a source of wisdom for the next wave of leaders God is moving into the missional field.

HUGH HALTER, Author of *The Tangible Kingdom* and
Flesh: Bringing the Incarnation Down to Earth

FOREWORD

by Mike Breen

In today's world, including within the church, the leaders we listen to are those who have built big things quickly. We admire big and we admire fast. We attend conferences where leaders of "mega" things teach us principles that promise that we, too, can achieve "mega" results if we could just get the right people on board and the right systems in place.

As well-meaning as these kinds of conferences intend to be, the quietly tragic result is that it leaves the vast majority of Christian leaders feeling like failures. When they don't see the "mega" results they were hoping for, when their group doesn't grow as quickly as they wanted, when half the people quit the small group after the first week, they struggle with the sneaking suspicion that maybe they don't really have what it takes to do this leadership thing with Jesus in his kingdom.

That's why Caesar's book is so vital right now. In these pages "you will discover the secret to starting out small and going (seemingly) slower—*and not feeling guilty about it.*"

And here's the cool thing: the reason you don't need to feel guilty about being small or slow is not because Jesus wants to give you a consolation prize or a participation ribbon. *It's because Jesus himself led by starting small and going (seemingly) slow.*

The reason this book is so needed right now is that *the paradoxical pathway of Jesus that actually produces the most fruit in the long run is almost the exact opposite of the advice most of us hear every day.* Small *is* big. Slow *is* fast. The title of this book is more than just a clever play on words. It's literally and vitally *true.* The processes that produce lots of quick results are not the same processes that produce the long-term fruitfulness that Jesus is wanting, the fruitfulness that he himself models for us and empowers us to imitate.

The growth curve of making disciples who make disciples actually *outpaces* the "mega" growth curve in the long run. As Caesar says in the book, in the end, multiplication wins! It creates an exponential equation that grows deeper and deeper even as it expands wider and wider.

To help us get started on the right foot, this book outlines the principles Jesus taught about the foundation of multiplication and making disciples. But it doesn't stop there. It also talks in detail about the practicalities of what that looks like from day to day. The whole book is laced with experience-drenched wisdom that will allow you to actually step into kingdom mission with Jesus in a practical way.

This is more vital than ever before, because we need to get back to doing ministry and leadership in the *way* of Jesus. So let's go for it, pursuing abundant fruitfulness in making disciples by starting small and going (seemingly) slow.

MIKE BREEN, Global Team Leader–3D Movements; author of *Building a Discipleship Culture* and *Leading Kingdom Movements*

ACKNOWLEDGMENTS

The things that I write about are born in experience, in community. They are birthed in my own family and then grow outward and are shared with others.

I am unimaginably thankful for the original Team K: my ever-gracious wife, Tina, who is the truest missionary I know, and my children — Caesar, Christin, and Justine — who love many and love well. The life and relationships that God has given us are amazing. What a gift you are! I am also grateful for the others who are now part of Team K by adoption or by association. You know who you are, and you continue to bless and model the gospel to me in incredible ways.

Thank you to all of those in Soma who have walked this journey with us for many years now. So much of what we learned together is in here.

Thanks to Mike Breen and Dave Rhodes for fresh wind in my sails and new wisdom and insight into this life as a family on mission.

Thanks to my agent and friend, Greg Johnson; my editor, Ryan Pazdur; and all the team at Zondervan for your continued hard work and support on this journey.

And finally, humble thanks to our amazing God, who would choose to use a messed-up kid from the Midwest to proclaim his incredible love and glory.

INTRODUCTION

Bigger. Faster. Louder.

That pretty much sums up the American way of life.

Isn't a bigger television, a bigger house, a bigger salary ... better than a smaller one?!

Wouldn't you want a faster car, a faster computer, or a faster resolution to a painful situation?

We all sort of intrinsically know that to get any attention in this world, in the market, or at the dinner table, we are going to have to be and live a little louder than the next guy.

That's how it works. That's how you get ahead, or grow things, or amass lots of ... whatever. Bigger, faster, louder sums it up pretty well in our culture.

Unfortunately, this pattern of thinking has seeped in and infiltrated our methods of being the church, making disciples, or even starting new faith communities. We live in a time when very few Christians have actually been discipled — much less know how to make disciples. And institutionally we seem to believe that in order to have a successful new church, it is best to start things off like a shotgun blast: have lots of people at an opening "event" (bigger is better), work hard to get to multiple services and/or locations (as fast as possible to justify the expenses we are incurring), and make sure you have enough marketing (louder!) to keep a steady stream of folks coming through the doors to add to the membership rolls. I know this to be true, because I spent years helping to promote and lead this type of "church growth."

But there is a huge problem with this way of thinking when it comes to the kingdom of God and the making of disciples. In all of these things — and it seems to go completely against our instinct — small is big, slow is fast, and multiplication wins.

Every time.

Jesus taught all of this in his "upside down" ways of the kingdom. Remember the parable of the mustard seed. It's a perfect illustration of *small is big.* Or consider Jesus choosing only a handful of close associates to train and really pour himself into for *three* years. Couple this with his final command to his disciples to go and make more disciples who would make disciples. Look what happened. The church's existence around the world today is proof of Jesus' teaching and methods having an explosive capability when empowered by his Spirit.

Small is big. Slow is fast.

It works this way personally as well. Stop and think for a moment. What areas of your life are you trying to change or grow in right now? Did you begin yesterday? The truth is that no one can master a new skill in a day. You can't learn to speak the Arabic language in a few weeks — it takes time! It's the little things done consistently over time that develop into habits and patterns. Nothing in our lives that has great value, substance, and nuance is integrated quickly into our lives.

It also works this way when building meaningful relationships and lasting community. We don't create lifelong friendships overnight. They take time, consistent investment, and sacrifice. Key conversations and activities over the long haul build trust and form true, loving, and open communities. We can't rush these things into existence. But we can lay careful groundwork and create the right environments for organic growth and eventually multiplication. It's exactly the same when it comes to making disciples and reproducing healthy families and communities that live on God's mission.

TIME FOR A SHIFT

If you are interested in developing leaders and want to see a movement of the gospel that saturates your neighborhood and your city, then it is time to apply some unconventional wisdom to your church. It's time to unleash the kinds of growth and influence that we see in the early New Testament church. And there are three key principles that defined those early years as that small community grew and developed.

Small is big. Slow is fast. And multiplication always wins.

Let's think about this in your own context. Imagine what it would look like in your neighborhood if you and your family, along with another fifteen to twenty people were living examples of the gospel: serving, loving, sharing the life of Jesus freely, naturally, with everyone. And what if that was multiplied into two or three communities? How would your city change if dozens of these gospel communities were scattered all over town?

This is the dream. But it is also a very real possibility. This is what Jesus promised us!

Maybe you have spent years or even decades *going* to church and now, for whatever reason, you want to dive a little deeper into the mix. You want to try and figure out how to *be* the church — for yourself, for your family, and for those you love and care about who have already voted "no" on the whole *going to church* thing.

Perhaps you are a "church planter" or are thinking of becoming one. If so, you may have spent time researching, planning, and possibly even launching a traditional Sunday service-focused "church." Now, after months or even years of hard work, you have burned through a ton of money, and you barely know the names of your own kids anymore. You have successfully started a church *service*, but at times you aren't sure if you actually have a new *church*! Where are the actual *disciples*? Where are the transformed lives?

I have written this book to encourage you and to challenge the status quo thinking about the church. I want you to know that you don't have to have the talents of a rock star or the wisdom of Yoda to effectively and naturally live a life on God's mission, making disciples who make disciples. You do not have to add a big list of new activities to your life to effectively make disciples. In fact, it is actually quite simple, though not easy. It is the everyday, ordinary things done with greater gospel intentionality that will make all the difference ... slowly, over time.

HOW WE ROLL

In this book you will discover the secret to starting out small and going (seemingly) slower — and not feeling guilty about it. You will learn to trust that when the right foundations are set, multiplication can occur, and it will always be "faster" and more successful in the long run. While this is not specifically a book about personal spiritual growth, we will begin with how you lead the person staring back at you in the mirror, how you personally lead a life that is on mission with God. We will dig deeply into how the good news of the gospel motivates us toward a lifestyle of discipleship. And I will focus on starting and leading healthy gospel communities that live on mission — starting with your own family and moving out from there.

God's extended family (we Christians, in the normal rhythms of life) is the context in which disciples are made and multiplied. We will take a look at an average week in the life of a regular family who is living with others on mission. I think you will be encouraged to see just how natural it can be to integrate God's mission into all of life.

I am not going to hide this from you: it is my hope that everyone who reads this book will share it with several others, starting in their home, and then begin to live the life that God created them to live. I believe God is waiting to fill our cities with gospel-centered communities that bring his life, love, and salvation to many. I envision an explosion of new missional churches that will become virtual engines for the creation and sending out of more and more disciples ... who in turn make more disciples.

Will you join God on his mission?

I know that sounds like a lot to take in, so I promise to break this down for you. We will start off with the basics and move step by step. At the end of each chapter I will challenge you to take small, slow action steps, and we'll check a few signposts of where you should be on the journey to living on mission.

And to be clear up front, none of this can be accomplished without the Spirit of God at work, so in every way, I encourage you to trust the Spirit of our missional God to guide you. This is *his* mission we are called to.

The pressure's off, but it's time to press on....

CHAPTER 1

LOOKING BACK TO MOVE FORWARD

Several years ago I was having the rockin'est year in business that I had ever had. Our publishing company was growing exponentially, and I had the financial freedom to finally bless my family with a few long-desired upgrades in life. I had quite a bit of time and the flexibility to travel internationally, doing some pretty amazing work in Africa and Asia by helping deliver the gospel and much-needed relief to those suffering religious persecution or pinned down under the weight of war.

It was a good time in my life in pretty much every way—all great.

That's when God stepped in and messed everything up.

At forty years of age, and with everything going perfectly (according to my sovereign plans), I heard God speak very clearly to me, telling me that I was to become a pastor. "A *what*, Lord?" It's not that God spoke to me audibly that day, but it was pretty close. The clarity with which I heard his voice, and the subsequent confirmations that happened almost daily, only clarified his call on my life.

"But I'm not a pastor!" I said to him. I had never been to Bible college or seminary. I had zero professional training. I had no desire to wear a suit, slick back my hair, and steer a pulpit every Sunday for the rest of my life. Besides, what church would hire me? Despite my objections, in faith I dutifully responded, "Yes, Father, I'll be a *pastor* ... if that's your will for my life. But you'll have to work out all of the business stuff I'm committed to, and oh yeah — show me *where* I'm supposed to pastor too."

Through a series of crazy moves that felt like miracles, within ninety days I was completely removed from my responsibilities within our company, was receiving a pretty fat severance check every month, and was now free as a bird to be a pastor. There was only one problem — I wasn't one yet. No one had called me anywhere or had yet offered me a position at a church. My wife, Tina, and I had been involved at a very large church in the Chicago suburbs for over nine years, and we were both super-involved in the local and international ministries of the church, but there were no job offers there, no one asking me to help the team "pastor up."

I know this, because I asked them.

Their laughter and the polite way they said, "No thanks, Caesar, you're probably not a good fit on our staff ... (*pat, pat on the back*)," left me with very few options. And it also left me wondering if I had just screwed up my family's life and driven us off a cliff.

Not sure what else to do, I set to work remodeling my basement and found that I had plenty of time to talk to my heavenly Dad about what all he was thinking. Ninety days later (again) to the date, I received a call. It was the executive pastor of our church, and he wanted to know if I was free to come in and have a talk with our senior pastor: "Jim wants to talk to you about that job that's opening up for a communications director ... it's a new pastoral position we're creating."

Boom! That's my opening ... Come on, Lord!

And it happened. I was hired on full-time, at my own local church, as the pastor overseeing all communications. I worked with a large staff and volunteer team. Soon I added the title of "Missions Pastor" to my job description and even got to preach on the *big stage* once in a while.

Real pastorin' stuff.

For the next three years I learned a lot about local ministry as I pastored in this church context. I will be forever grateful to God and the staff I worked with during those years. My life, character, and theology were shaped in profound ways during that time, and yet I still wondered, was *this* the call I had heard from God? Was I living a transformed and eternally purposed life?

After a few years, I began to chafe a bit, wondering if Jesus had died on the cross so that a few chosen people in a church service could "do" the ministry while pretty much everyone else just sat there, passively and silently watching. Was this what God had in mind? Was this the hope we had for growth and maturity as a follower of Jesus? Was the highest goal for most of my friends to become an usher in the church building ... to someday *ush* with the best of them?

Around this time, I was doing some traveling overseas, and I read and re-read the book of Acts. A very different picture of the church emerged, one that was strikingly similar to what I was seeing and experiencing as I traveled outside the United States. The way that Jesus taught and lived with his disciples, and how they in turn lived, looked a whole lot more like what I was seeing in Africa and India than it did in my own life and church back home.

I wondered what it would be like to live in real community with others, not just saying hello to them once a week and shaking hands. I wondered what it would look like to intentionally disciple each other to greater faith in Jesus, living together as God's missionary family, here in my own neighborhood.

There was one huge problem in all of this.

I had zero *not-yet-believing* friends. In fact, I hardly even knew my neighbors.[1] I was too darn busy pulling off all the programs that went on throughout the week (after week after week) at the church building.

RECORD SCRATCH . . . FULL STOP

Wait a minute, that doesn't make sense! If I and a handful of other pastors and leaders in the church are supposed to be role models for the rest of our people, showing them how to live and make disciples as Jesus did, shouldn't pastors have loads of not-yet-believing friends? Shouldn't we be rock-star disciple makers, living the same way Jesus and his disciples did?

What I learned was that the way the disciples of Jesus lived was not only in stark contrast to his own culture, but was upside down compared to everything else at that time, both Jewish *and* pagan. A pattern of teaching and living began to emerge that was profound, yet much simpler than I had seen or experienced in my own life. There was an "all in" nature to life in the kingdom of God, but the process for getting in and living out this life was somehow ... uncomplicated, less pressured and mustered up, less programmed. Jesus would hang out with and teach his disciples through short, simple stories called parables, life lessons that opened up their hearts and minds to a new way of living. A new way of being.

I wanted that. Everybody wants that. Or so I thought.

MISSIONAL, HERE I COME

I began to hear people using a term that described the life of Jesus and his disciples—the way those first believers lived, as well as those who live like missionaries today. The word was "missional." *Missional* carries with it the idea that our lives should be radically oriented around the mission of Jesus, the same mission that he sent his disciples to replicate—making disciples who make disciples, as a family of missionaries, together. As we began to learn more about what it meant to live this way, Tina and I decided we would begin to gather up some of our closest Christian friends to eat meals together and discuss what it would look like for us to start living as a *missional community*, treating each other like family and inviting those whom God would (hopefully) call us to disciple to hang out with us and walk more closely with Jesus.

Maybe you've never heard the word *missional* before. Let me explain. "Missional" isn't a form of church. It's a label we give to the qualitative or descriptive aspect of how a church actually lives. To put it simply, it's about how much like Jesus people become and how much they influence, woo, and transform the culture in which they are placed. In other words, how "missional" you are is largely determined by the extent to which you and your community model the life, activities, and words of Jesus.[2]

Sounds good, right? Our friends all thought so too. We were all excited to be missional, to live as a missional community. Excited, that is, until things progressed to where we moved beyond our weekly meal and discussion about *being* missional to heading out and building new relationships, serving those in need in our city ... actually *going* to make disciples. That's when everyone recoiled a bit.

"Hmmm ... This would mean that my schedule would have to change quite a bit. We're just too busy right now."

"Maybe in the winter, once we get past all of our kids' sports activities. We'll see then."

That's when it all fell apart. We pretty quickly disbanded our little "band of brothers" and, greatly discouraged, decided that this just would not work in the suburbs of Chicago.

I'll dig deeper into this experience later, but for now the point is that not everyone who was a Christian was willing to jump right into this new "missional lifestyle" with us. They all agreed that this was biblical, but their existing preconceptions of Christianity, the church, and their own priorities acted as a huge gravitational pull backward, away from a life where the priority and focus was living on mission with God. Apparently we still had a lot to learn about how best to implement Jesus' methods of making disciples.

A PATTERN AND A PROMISE

There is a reason Jesus lived and taught in the ways he did. He wasn't random or cleverly trying to adapt to the local customs of his day. Yes, his methods were rooted in real life and they were immersed into his culture, but there was something far more eternal and subversive going on. Jesus was on his Father's mission, restoring all things to the way he originally created them to be. His life and teachings both provide the example for us and open up a new possibility—for people to once again live in a close relationship with God under his rule and reign. Jesus taught in parables that offered his disciples (and us) a pattern and a promise for life in the kingdom: "For who hath despised the day of small things?"[3]

In Luke 13 we encounter Jesus explaining how the good news of the kingdom—what we commonly refer to as the gospel—works itself out, starting with the basic principle *small is big*.

> Jesus asked, "What is the kingdom of God like? What shall I compare it to? It is like a mustard seed, which a man took and planted in his garden. It grew and became a tree, and the birds perched in its branches."[4]

The pattern here is clear and simple. This new kingdom restoration doesn't start off big, with everyone jumping on board. Notice that Jesus tells us that the little mustard seed is first planted in the man's *own* garden. After it is planted, it grows into something larger, something that others can find their place in. There are many small steps on the journey to a kingdom life lived with Jesus on his mission. All of your steps will be baby steps at first.

The promise is also clear. After the good news of the kingdom takes root and changes your own heart, Jesus promises it will expand outward to include others. The seemingly small first steps you take to cultivate growth in your own life *will* grow over time and have a larger effect on others.

We are not called to build elaborate, structured programs and systems and then expect lots of people to come on in and fill them up for us. Instead, we are to plant small (gospel) seeds that will eventually grow into changed lives, changed families, and changed communities.

Small is big. That's the first kingdom principle that Jesus taught. But it wasn't the only one. Continuing with his disciples, Jesus taught them another kingdom code: *slow is fast.*

> Again he [Jesus] asked, "What shall I compare the kingdom of God to? It is like yeast that a woman took and mixed into about sixty pounds of flour until it worked all through the dough."[5]

The pattern: Like yeast, a catalyst for change and growth, the gospel begins to affect our lives slowly at first, igniting a change within us that influences every aspect of our existence.

The promise: The good news of the kingdom is about more than just our afterlife, what happens to us when we die. Christianity is about more than sin, heaven, and hell. Jesus' kingdom rule and reign is present *now*, and it transforms everything about us. It changes our perspectives and priorities, our motives and methods. Living on God's mission of making disciples is about small shifts in belief and practice that over time make a big difference. Just as a ball of dough takes time to rise, we need to be patient with God's process of change and growth in our hearts and lives.

MULTIPLICATION WINS!

There is an underlying principle in both of these parables, a goal that these two principles lead to: *multiplication*. The good news of Jesus' kingdom rule and reign is not just about the small changes in your life that lead to transformation over time, nor is it simply a matter of taking time and having the patience to do the right things. Both of these parables teach us that life in the kingdom *always* leads to multiplication. And multiplication *always* beats out hard work, sacrifice, and big goals and dreams, eventually changing the world.

It is interesting to me that in Matthew's gospel, right after he records these two parables, he shows Jesus continuing on with back-to-back parables on how valuable the kingdom of God is:

> "The kingdom of heaven is like treasure hidden in a field. When a man found it, he hid it again, and then in his joy went and sold all he had and bought that field.
>
> "Again, the kingdom of heaven is like a merchant looking for fine pearls. When he found one of great value, he went away and sold everything he had and bought it."[6]

After sharing these two short parables, Jesus wraps up his teaching time with the disciples by telling them a final parable about some fishermen who let down their nets to catch "all kinds of fish." This likely would have reminded them of an earlier time when Jesus commanded Peter and his buddies to throw out their nets after a long night of fishing.[7] When they pulled the nets back into their boat, they were overflowing with fish to the point of breaking! The fishermen were amazed at this miracle, and it's almost as if Jesus is saying to them, "That's how I roll!" He wants them to understand that *the kingdom life will always lead to expansion and abundance.* He is saying to them, "Healthy things grow. They multiply. And that's how God has ordered all of life. And I am going to show you how to live this way and teach others as well."

In a later chapter we will take a closer look at how this principle applies to life in practical ways. You can and must learn how to seed multiplication into every area of life and mission if you are to truly live a kingdom life, one that "grows" to include many others.

CRACKING THE NUT

What about my own story? Well, a year or so after our failed attempt at starting a missional community, God called my family to pack up and move out to Tacoma, Washington, to join our dear friends, Jeff and Jayne Vanderstelt, on a new adventure.[8] The Vanderstelts had moved out to Tacoma to help start new churches, churches that more closely resembled the kinds of communities we had been reading about in the book of Acts. These were churches that followed a different pattern, one that was in line with this new recalibration of Jesus' teachings in our minds and hearts.

Jeff and Jayne had actually been involved in that first small circle of friends who had never cracked the nut on living missionally, and they were determined to give it another try. Tacoma is a city that has very few Christians, a place where a tiny percentage of the population even "goes to church," and as we settled into our new neighborhood we asked the question, "How would Jesus live *here*?"

God's answer to our question was to birth a new community that we called Soma. We started simply—a small group of people doing very normal, everyday stuff, but with the intentional commitment to live as Jesus would live if he was living *our* life. We regularly ate meals together and served one another and the needs of our families, friends, and neighbors. And we learned to apply the good news of the gospel to different areas of life. Soon everything began to change for us, and we experienced growth. As I said earlier, healthy things *always* grow.

Out of that first "core group" community we sent four groups of brothers and sisters into their own neighborhoods with a commitment to continue in the same rhythms we all had been following. It wasn't always easy, but these communities grew. The same rhythms of life — the ways we shared meals, served, and learned together — were now being repeated in the lives of others as well. Before too long, some of those new missional communities birthed groups of their own. Over the next several years our Soma family grew into dozens of these "gospel-centered communities" all over town. Today it is hard to find a person in Tacoma who hasn't heard of Soma or met someone who is involved in a missional community. Our intention was never to become well known, but when the good news is lived out in a community, it is something people will notice and talk about.

What we experienced over time was that when we focused on small yet important and ordinary parts of life, submitting them to Jesus, seeking to build his kingdom instead of our own, everything began to change. Not only did others notice, but they wanted to be a part of what we were doing. It was not uncommon to hear friends say to us, "I'm not really into the church thing or religion, but I love you guys and want to be a part of whatever this is!"

Small is big, slow is fast, and multiplication wins.

ON EARTH AS IT IS IN HEAVEN

All of this is bigger than you might think. What I'm talking about in this book is not just an alternative way to "do church." This missional lifestyle, with its intentional focus on God's kingdom and allowing his rule over every area of our life, has eternal implications. Jesus' life—his teachings, death, and resurrection—was all part of God's eternal plan to restore everything back to the way he originally created it to be. Relationships between God and human beings, and relationships between people, are being brought back to their intended righteousness—their *right-use-ness*—all to display God's glory, to show the world what he is really like.

God is restoring our relationships, our marriages, our families, our worldview, our work ethic, our sexual orientation, our identity, and every other part of who we are back to the way he desires them to be. And that only happens when the gospel gets in and changes and heals our hearts, displacing the lies we have believed about God and ourselves.

Those changes may seem small at first. We may wonder if they are really making any difference at all. Restoration happens slowly, but as we walk with Jesus and invite others to do the same, we begin to see just how far this can reach. We begin to understand God's vision and his plan for changing the world through individual and community transformation and the power of multiplication.

As Christians we can continue to falsely assume that our highest calling is to attend a weekly church service and serve in a few church programs. We can continue to live as "good Christians" who embrace the American Dream and squeeze in some time to serve Jesus when and if it fits our schedule. But there is another story we need to hear, one that doesn't jibe with the tale we've grown up believing: The kingdom of God has come, and our King desires to have our entire life. He doesn't just give us a ticket to a happy afterlife. He wants us to be a part of his work today. We were created and saved to live with Jesus, and we are empowered by his own Spirit to be part of his restoration of all things.

> *The mission of the church is eternal. Its origin is in eternity and its destination is eternity.*
>
> —R. C. SPROUL

Why settle for comfort and conformity when you were destined for glory?

TRANSFORMED

The kingdom of God comes to bear in our lives when we live under the rule and reign of God and his ways instead of our own. The goal of Jesus' life was to glorify his Father. He did this by living the life he saw his Father live, by displaying his Father's heart, life, and reality.[9]

Like a lot of things in life, when it comes to our faith, we default to thinking that we must *do* something in order to *be* someone. But don't miss this: if you have put your hope and trust in Jesus, you have become a disciple. That is your new transformed identity. A disciple is someone who has reoriented his or her life around another to become, in essence, who that person is. Sure, as always, who we are does lead to what we do and how we live, but at the heart of being a disciple of Jesus is a desire to be like him.

Jesus showed his disciples how to be like him and then sent them out to in turn make more disciples. The Father's heart and life were magnified through Jesus' life and then further multiplied through his disciples.

And now through our lives.

Here are a few more examples I see of things that Jesus taught and modeled to his followers. Viewed through the lens of *small is big, slow is fast*, they can lead to great multiplication and transformation in our lives — and in our communities as well. Let me paraphrase a few of these teachings and the powerful implications they carry.

Jesus taught that we are to live radically generous lives: "If someone asks for your shirt, give them your coat too!"[10]

Can you imagine what would happen if — little by little — we began to treat all of our possessions as kingdom tools and provisions to show others God's love and generosity? We could live with such freedom from consumerism, enjoying God's blessings but not being controlled by them. These concrete expressions of generosity would also show others that God is for and not against them as they experience his blessings delivered through the hands of his people.

Or consider the way we lead others. Leadership, in the kingdom of God, looks like "servantship." Jesus told those who followed him, "I didn't come to be served, but to serve others; now go and do the same."[11] What an upside-down model for leading people! Taking on the posture of a slave or servant is startling to those around you because it is so radically different from what they are used to. But this posture of serving others builds trusting relationships that cause people to pursue you and desire to know more of why you would live and lead this way.

Small acts of service can have eternal ramifications. Jesus said to his disciples, "When you open up a place at the table, offer someone a drink, or visit another in bondage, you're blessing me and accomplishing my eternal plans."[12]

Service is not always a big project or program that takes lots of planning to pull off. There are opportunities to serve others all around us—times when we step in, and one thing leads to another, and God is seen for who he really is. While no one thing you do may seem like a big deal, in God's sovereign economy we know that he is working it all out for his glory. Just a little faith in God's power can overcome any obstacle. Jesus likened it to telling a mountain to fling itself into the ocean ... and it does![13]

So often we are afraid to start on a great journey because we fear we will not finish or be successful. We will not speak the truth out of confusion or concern over our own lack of knowledge. But Jesus taught his disciples to trust in his great power and not their own—starting small if need be, because even our little faith in his enormous ability can accomplish much.

Jesus is not a King who can be followed in your spare time. God is not interested in our leftovers. And not everyone will follow you into the radical life of Jesus. But some will. Start with your own family and close friends and trust that God will show you which people he has chosen for you, those he has called you to walk alongside and disciple.

There are many, many more examples that we could dig into, but you see the pattern. Now, when you read the Gospels and the book of Acts, look for how often this same pattern of *small is big, slow is fast, multiplication wins* shows up.

YOU'RE DOING *WHAT* EXACTLY AND *WHY*?

Whenever we start to make a move spiritually that doesn't look like what we grew up doing or are familiar with, it's natural to feel a bit of skepticism. Doubts surface, from others, and in our own hearts and minds as well. "Maybe I'm crazy to think that we could actually live this way!" Initially you might struggle to embrace the patterns and rhythms of life, living how Jesus did with his disciples.

In some ways I have always had this "removed and otherworldly" perspective on how Jesus and his disciples lived and made disciples, thinking how huge and impossible that must be for us who live now in "modern times." But when I actually read what the Bible says, it almost looks too normal—too simple to be true. It seems that Jesus and his disciples lived really ordinary lives, but because of the mission they were on, and the faith in the power of the Holy Spirit that they had, amazing things were happening.

Maybe the voices of others are popping up in your head or, at times, your ears ... "I don't know, brother, this all sounds good and biblical I suppose, but good luck! I don't know how you'll ever get your family or anyone else to go along with this stuff for long. Everyone's just too dang busy." Or maybe you hear, "Listen, sis, if this is how we were really supposed to be living our lives all the time, our church and every other church in the world would be teaching this to us and our pastors would be totally living this out, right? Things are just different here now in this day and in our world."

I want to encourage you to push through this. A life lived on mission with God, where your focus and priorities are reoriented around making disciples who make disciples, does not happen like flipping on a light switch and suddenly become a reality in your day-to-day experience. The early church was made up of very real and ordinary flesh-and-blood people. They weren't a fluke or a historical anomaly. The life they experienced in community together didn't happen overnight. And just as we saw with Jesus and his followers, you will need to start small, go slowly, and learn to trust God himself to guide you.

We really do get to live this way.

Small is Big: What small, yet maybe profound thing did you take away from this chapter? Write it down. What little "mustard seed" is starting to grow in the field of your heart now? Ask God to give you the courage where needed to begin to live in light of these truths.

Slow is Fast: What is one thing you can start doing that would not create too much disruption to your schedule, but would start to head you down the path of discipleship as a way of life? Commit this to prayer, tell someone else about it, and start tomorrow!

Multiplication Wins: Who do you know that you could begin to talk and pray with about these things? Ask God to show you who he might have you begin to live with as part of a missional community in the near future.

Signpost: A journey begins with a first step. At this point you are looking over the maps and "Kingdom trade routes" that Jesus established. I encourage you to believe what is true of you now: if you are a Christian, you are a part of God's family and commissioned to bear the family name and be a missionary servant and a disciple who makes disciples in all of life. This is a part of your *identity* now. Being leads to doing. Let your true identity begin to shape the things that God has for you to do.

CHAPTER 2

ME, MYSELF, AND MINE

I did a lot of traveling internationally when my kids were younger. It was not uncommon for God to take me into a war zone or the aftermath of a natural disaster for weeks at a time. The things I saw, smelled, tasted—and sometimes ate—left profound impressions on my life in regard to having an entitlement mentality. Fortunately, seeing people with so little means of support (or none) made me a more grateful person, at least for a while, and I wanted my family to truly understand this and embrace God's abundant grace poured into our life.

When you experience radical differences in lifestyles and the expectations of other people who are at a similar age and stage of life as you are, it can really throw you for a loop and cause you to do some crazy recalibrating.

I started noticing how much complaining we all did back home. One regular source of grumbling was around the dinner table. My kids were around thirteen, eleven, and nine years old at the time, and even though my wife is a seriously awesome cook, they often didn't want to eat what she made and set on the table.

At one point, after returning from a trip overseas, I decided I had had enough.

"That's it, this has to stop! Don't you kids know how lucky you are to have food like this?! Do you know that two-thirds of the people living on this planet would be *stoked* if they just had beans and rice to eat today? Just once a day ... not three meals. [I'm probably shouting a little at this point.] I have been with so many children who have had nothing to eat for days or even weeks, and they would be *thrilled* to have just a little beans and rice to eat!" Yikes.

So I concocted a plan that my wife went along with. For the next thirty days our family would eat *nothing* but beans and rice for dinner. That's it. The kids could still have their normal breakfast of Cheerios and toast or whatever, they could eat their school lunches, but at dinnertime it would be nothing but beans and rice for an entire month. Then ... maybe they—I mean *we*—would learn to be a little more thankful for what we have to eat around here.

Awesome, right?

The kids didn't think so, yet they had no choice but to go along for the ride. And so it went, at least until we were twelve days into our little experiment in attitude adjustment. I came home from work on that twelfth day, and my wife was just getting ready to set out dinner. I noticed that she was *not* serving beans and rice. What?!

"Why are we not having beans and rice for dinner tonight? We're not even halfway through the month!"

Tina explained. Today was our daughter Christin's birthday. As was our regular family tradition, she got to pick what we ate for dinner—her birthday, her choice. "Yeah, but not this time! We're doing the beans and rice thing. No way!" I objected. But it was too late. The food was cooked. The promise had been made. We shared a meal of broccoli chicken divan,[1] followed by birthday cake with eleven blazing candles and chocolate ice cream.

Now, I have to admit that even though Tina had been pretty creative in making a variety of different versions of beans and rice so far, this was a welcome break in the action. But, not one to go back on my ruthless quest to "be more thankful," I reinstituted the experiment by *starting over* for another full thirty days. So in the end we ended up eating beans and rice for thirty days *plus* the original twelve.

Alrighty!

The kids about freaked out, and I ended up looking like a bit of a tyrant as a father, but I have to say that the experience changed our family in some pretty cool ways. We really did become much more thankful for the blessings God had given our family. We talked long and hard about why some people have so much while others seem to get much less. And to this day, my kids will eat *anything* that is put in front of them. Anything.

Sometimes we need to stare our self-centeredness right in the face in order to truly see it. We miss everyday opportunities for growth and provisions of grace if we're not looking for them. God can shape our lives in some pretty amazing ways once he gets our attention.

By the way, I still order beans and rice whenever I eat tacos. My kids, not so much.

FOLLOW ME

The idea of living like a family on God's mission is at the center of the gospel itself. Our submission to God *as God*, or lack thereof, is what sin and rebellion are all about. Who is going to be Lord in your life? What will be the central and dominant motivation of our hearts and why? Whose life is ultimately on display and preeminent?

We often think that Jesus simply walked up to people, called them to drop everything they were doing and follow him, and BOOM! everyone did. But according to Luke, there were also times when Jesus called people to live the kingdom life and they gave him a bunch of "me first" excuses. These were reasons to refuse Jesus, excuses designed to look good and allow them to continue building their own kingdoms ... at least for a little while longer.

> As they were walking along the road, a man said to him, "I will follow you wherever you go."
> Jesus replied, "Foxes have dens and birds have nests, but the Son of Man has no place to lay his head."
> He said to another man, "Follow me."
> But he replied, "Lord, first let me go and bury my father."
> Jesus said to him, "Let the dead bury their own dead, but you go and proclaim the kingdom of God."
> Still another said, "I will follow you, Lord; but first let me go back and say goodbye to my family."
> Jesus replied, "No one who puts a hand to the plow and looks back is fit for service in the kingdom of God."[2]

The first guy Jesus meets reminds me of myself. I'm one of those people who is super ready to jump on that new thing for God, sign up, and get after it. "I will follow you wherever you go, Jesus." Sounds good, right? Well, it seems that Jesus knew that man's heart (as he knows mine), and he realized that like many people, this guy had not really counted the cost of discipleship.

It's as if Jesus is saying to him, "You claim to be ready to follow me anywhere, but are you willing to give up the material comforts in your life?"

As far as we can tell, Jesus never owned a home. He seemed to eat whatever was offered him, often going without food. And how did others see him? He was hated by the religious elite, ridiculed by those from his hometown, and frequently doubted by his closest followers. That's how our Lord lived. That's how the King of Kings chose to live for his Father's glory. Talk about an entitlement killer! Can we be his disciples and expect—much less demand—more comfort, wealth, or status than Jesus?

What kinds of decisions are we asked to make before following Jesus into a life of radical discipleship in community with others? What will we lay on the line and let God decide?

ME FIRST

The next fella that Jesus called to follow him was on board, ready to follow, but he had one thing left to do: *"Lord, first let me go and bury my father."*[3] Was this wrong? Was it a bad thing for this man to want to go care for his father? It's hard for us to understand Jesus' response to this man without knowing more about the cultural norms at that time. It's most likely that the man was not asking to attend his father's funeral, as if he had just died yesterday. What he was really saying was, *"After my father has died, and I've completed my duties as his son, I'll receive my inheritance; then I'll come and be your disciple."*

So the real issue wasn't, *"Lord . . . give me an extra day."* It was, *"Lord . . . me first."* The other words he spoke were just a smoke-screen for his real desire to put himself first. Procrastination and wanting to feather his future nest *before* being obedient to the call of discipleship exposed his heart.

How did Jesus respond to the man? Let me paraphrase. Jesus said: "There are certain things that a spiritually dead person can do just as well as followers of mine. But there are other things in life that only my own can do. Don't spend your life doing what those in the world could have done just as well. Let the focus of your life and energy be to advance my kingdom and mission."

You see, the seemingly legitimate concerns of life can become sinful when we let them take priority over the interests of Jesus. "Kingdom first" is the word Jesus gives to this man—and to all he calls to follow him. So what are some of the things in your own life that could potentially delay or keep you from living fully on mission with God today? Jobs, careers, schooling, recreation, and retirement—all of these seem like important things—and they are! But we're as guilty as the man in this story if we put these things on the *me first* list, ahead of God's call on our lives.

SANCTIFIED DISTRACTIONS

The third man says to Jesus, *"I will follow you, Lord; but first let me go back and say goodbye to my family."*[4] Okay, if you've been paying attention, you probably just noticed the *me first* part.

Not a good start.

What's wrong with a guy wanting to go back and hug his family and say goodbye? I mean, come on now, Jesus! Why would saying goodbye to your folks get you labeled as "not fit for service in the kingdom of God"? Jesus' response to the man about having "put your hand to the plow" and then looking back sounds like pretty heavy stuff.

So let's unpack it a bit more. Jesus is saying that once a person has tasted his love, grace, peace, and forgiveness — once we have come to know him — there should be no comparison to make, nothing better in life. How can a person still look back over their shoulder at the stuff of this world and compare that to him? And if we do that ... if the worldly stuff still looks so good to us that it's on the same list as Jesus, on the same shelf of priority in our hearts, then we will never be of much use in doing the work of his kingdom. Ouch!

I think Jesus' heart in all of this is, "I want my disciples to have their priorities straight! You're going to have to love me more than your families, friends, and fun. No more self-centered life. You will have to put me above everyone else to be my disciple. No looking back."[5]

Just in case you're wondering if Jesus' call is really this drastic of a shift in lifestyle and priorities, later in Luke's account Jesus goes on to say, "If anyone comes to me and does not hate father and mother, wife and children, brothers and sisters — yes, even their own life — such a person cannot be my disciple."[6]

This one is a killer for a lot of people. Many of us have been raised to believe that our families should come first in life. Again, Jesus is not saying that we should go all lunatic and hateful on our families and friends, but he calls us to evaluate where they are on our list of affections as his disciples. In my experience, getting this one right takes real dependence on the Holy Spirit or I tend to tip off one side or the other of this boat.

From a gospel perspective, our *me first* attitude and misplaced priorities raise a form of consumerism and are anti–kingdom of God. It's our own attempt to search out a self-guided, self-obtained fulfillment, pleasure, identity, value, and in many cases, community. All of this, for us as Jesus followers, is supposed to be found in him!

To get you started working through all of this in your own heart, ask yourself, "What are some of the relationships that I tend to put before God's kingdom and his righteousness?" Think about the ones you would normally skip over and legitimize as "good and right." You have them, and so do I, and they sound something like "Once I take care of this one thing, I'll get back to a life of discipleship." The problem is, that "one thing" never goes away. What are the "good" things in your life that tend to take priority over Jesus and his call?

You might also think about the distractions in your life — family drama, seeking your parent's approval, any marital strife, or if you are single, the search for a spouse. If you are a parent, it might be that your kids are your idols and you are always trying to keep up with their sports and do what "good parents" do.

Your list of legitimate "distractions" may be different from others', but anything you treat as a sacred cow is probably something you need to talk to Jesus about. He said, "In the same way, those of you who do not give up everything you have cannot be my disciples."[7]

You're probably reeling a bit from thinking through that list. Tough stuff, I know. But there is good news. The gospel works to deliver us from the *me first* lifestyle that we, as sinful and self-absorbed humans, inherited from our first parents, Adam and Eve. If you are used to a "weekly attendance" mindset when you think about church, and you view the rest of the week as "mine," real change has to occur. And it starts in the heart.

HEART CHANGE

In many ways, all of this is a call to die to *self*. It begins by simplifying your life as God rearranges your priorities and you spend more and more of your time living with God's mission at the center of our life. As Dietrich Bonhoeffer said,

> When Christ calls a man, He bids him come and die. It may be a death like that of the first disciples who had to leave home and work to follow Him, or it may be a death like Luther's, who had to leave the monastery and go out into the world. But it is the same death every time — death in Jesus Christ, the death of the old man at his call.[8]

One time a group of us were at a refuge camp in Sudan delivering food and aid to people who were literally near starvation. Mothers holding their skeletal children *begged* us for more food, but we could only give a predetermined amount to each family. Some of these poor, scared parents became angry at the size of the rations. But it was all that we had. All we could hope was that this food would hold them over until the next relief could arrive.

It seemed odd that even though we had flown halfway around the world to try to help these people, at great personal risk and expense, they were not all that grateful. God spoke to me about this, saying, "Do you think I brought you here to hand out (my) food so that folks would be pleased with you? You'll find that often when you serve others, they are not necessarily that happy or thankful. I sent you here to love them. And when you do, you are really showing love to me. And my priorities. Trust me with the results. I love you."

That changed me forever. I felt freed to serve and love, living out God's mission knowing that he loved me and that he was sending us, wherever we found ourselves, to show others what our loving Father is like. And to be honest, it was so much less about "doing" and much, much more about "being" and trusting.

C. S. Lewis once wrote,

> Christ says, "Give me All. I don't want so much of your time and so much of your money and so much of your work: I want you. I have not come to torment your natural self, but to kill it. No half-measures are any good. I don't want to cut off a branch here and a branch there, I want to have the whole tree down. I don't want to drill the tooth, or crown it, but to have it out. Hand over the whole natural self, all the desires which you think innocent as well as the ones you think wicked—the whole outfit. I will give you a new self instead. In fact, I will give you myself: my own shall become yours."[9]

Leading my family on mission, as a way of life, needed to start with my own heart. And God had gone to great lengths to get my attention.

I'm listening!

BUT I LIKE WHAT I LIKE

I've learned that old habits of schedule and comfort are hard to break. When it comes to leading yourself and your own family on mission, you have to look at it more like "weaning off" than "pulling the scab."

When our kids turned two years old, my wife and I decided that we would quit buying them new pacifiers. When the last one was lost or just got too nasty to use anymore, that was it. No more "binky" (as we called it). We would wean them off the object they had come to love, something that had given them great comfort, but was no longer good for them.

A few months after our third child, Justine, was born, we caught her older sister, Christin, (who was around two and a half years old) hiding behind the couch, just sucking away on her baby sister's new pacifier that she had swiped. She was like a drug addict getting a fix! Poor thing. Tina took her to the grocery store, let her pick out one last pacifier of her choosing, and explained to her that when this one was lost, that was it. She was a big girl now, and she would have to move on.

I am happy to report that Christin, who recently got married, no longer sucks on a binky.

COUNT THE COST

Why do I share this? The point is that we will need to be patient with ourselves—and others—in this process of change. Small is big, and slow is fast. This is especially true for those who were never really discipled or "apprenticed" in their faith in community with others. Ask God to show you things you may need to "die to" as well as new attitudes and rhythms you need to embrace. This is an important step, but it doesn't happen overnight. You've got to start by counting the cost of discipleship before heading out into open waters.

"Suppose one of you wants to build a tower. Won't you first sit down and estimate the cost to see if you have enough money to complete it? For if you lay the foundation and are not able to finish it, everyone who sees it will ridicule you, saying, 'This person began to build and wasn't able to finish.' "[10]

To get you started thinking about this in practical ways, here are some things that my wife and I found we needed to address when we were starting out. Some of these may need to be "placed on the altar" and given to God for him to reshape and use as he chooses.

- Mealtimes

- Your budget

- Personal time

- Your home

- Where you live

- Where you work, your job and income level

- Whom your kids play with

- Bedtime for you and your children

- What you do on holidays, and with whom

- How many activities your kids are involved in

- Time with extended family (which can conflict with schedules for being in community or out serving, as at the time of a family party or celebration)

- The opinions others have of us (such as our perfectly clean house, our cooking skills, our kids' behavior)

DEALING WITH MY "STUFF" PROBLEM

After living in community for a while in Tacoma, I met an older couple, not yet retired, but getting close to that stage of life. They were really cool folks who loved food, wine, and riding motorcycles. What's not to like? I thought they would be a perfect couple to start up a missional community (MC) in their neighborhood. When we talked to them about discipleship and mission, they were quick to assure us that they *already* lived this way and had been praying and looking for just such a church community to be a part of. Awesome!

I went with another leader to their house to have lunch and answer a few questions they had. They live in a beautiful home, decorated to the max. It had leather furniture, nice artwork and technology, and was all around a very cool place. We were enjoying a pleasant lunch, chatting away as this couple told us how "missional" they were.

We asked them about their neighbors, which ones they knew well, how it was going in building relationships with the parents and kids who lived around them. The wife replied first: "Oh, we don't really know any of our neighbors. We've never had any of them over." *Hmmm, how could this be?* I thought to myself. They just spent the last hour or so telling us about how they live like missionaries. That's weird.

I suggested to this couple that I have found that parents with kids are sort of "low-hanging fruit" when it comes to making friends and serving our neighbors. They usually have very obvious needs and are pretty open to relationships. Maybe the wife could become sort of the neighborhood Granny and love up on these kids after school as a way of serving the parents who worked.

"No way!" she exclaimed. "I don't want those kids running around in my house! They'll make a mess and break everything." My heart sank. We realized we had exposed an idol. We tried to talk to her about her concerns and how we all were learning to love people more than our possessions. (I could certainly speak from experience on that one!) The couple said they would pray about it—a nice Christian dodge—and told us they would see us that weekend at the Sunday gathering.

While this couple hung out around the fringes of our community for a few more months, they never really engaged in mission in their neighborhood. Eventually, they left us to be part of a church of people "more our own age." The whole experience saddened me, but it wasn't the last time we would encounter this. Unfortunately, it's something that we have run into many times in various forms. As was the case with Jesus, as he called individuals to leave behind their priorities, dreams, relationships, and possessions to follow him, not everyone will follow. Not everyone will want to answer the call. Please don't think this had anything to do with their age.

It didn't.

It had *everything* to do with their hearts and where their treasures lay.

WHAT DO *YOU* WANT?

As you come to the end of this chapter, you might be thinking to yourself, "Well, I guess self-denial and pain are really what this Christian life is all about. Unless I *hate* what I am doing and suffer through it all, it must not be from God. If I enjoy my life, I must be on the wrong track." However, doing what we *love*, regardless of the cost or sacrifice, never feels like a burden, but a privilege.

Think about raising kids, training in sports, studying for an exam, dieting, and so on. If the object of our "suffering" is what or who we love the most, then our perspective on all of this is changed. Then it is not a burden or a sacrifice, but something we *get* to do out of love.

A friend of mine[11] once said to me, "We all do exactly what we want to do every day."

What do you want the most?

Small is Big: What are the things that you and your family might currently love more than God's glory and his mission? Be honest! Prayerfully write down everything that the Spirit shines a light on in your heart.

Slow is Fast: From the list you made, what things need to be first to go ... to be set aside before you can really begin to live in a community on mission? This week ask the Holy Spirit to guide you into new rhythms with new motivations.

Multiplication Wins: Remember, starting to live life on mission takes time. Don't think of all of this like a big pile of things that need to change instantly, but more like adding layers of understanding and growth as you progress. Let the good news of Jesus' life given for you transform your understanding and priorities.

Signpost: This is the part of the journey where you, and those closest to you, will need to take a serious look at the things in your life that can and may derail you from the mission. Ask yourself if you are really ready to have God radically reorient your life around being and making disciples of Jesus. Your head may answer "yes," but your heart may still be lagging behind.

CHAPTER 3

GOSPEL MOTIVATION

Dinner parties at our house are a blast, especially when Tina is at the helm. Tina embodies hospitality and also happens to be an amazing cook. You can ask anyone who knows her. She is famous for her gracious ways and culinary skills, making everyone around feel like part of the family. That's especially awesome for someone like me, who is not the best cook but can unintentionally enlist everyone to my latest cause without their even knowing it.

We make a good team. She loves 'em up, I sign 'em up.

That's what we were doing when we first started trying to live this missional existence with some of our friends back in the Midwest. Remember how I shared that several years ago when we had gathered a small group of friends together, we began having meals and discussing what it would be like to live as a missional community? We started all of this via dinner parties that always included a friend or couple who were not-yet believers and then tried to cross-pollinate our relationships with them and those in our little group. Those were fun times, but netted little forward movement for any of us toward a better knowledge of the gospel or a deeper relationship with Jesus.

So I started to initiate some simple opportunities for us and our new friends to go and serve others in the community. I wanted us to start living like disciples, leading others (and ourselves) to walk in the ways of Jesus, applying the good news along the way.

Intentionality. That's what I was after.

But as I shared these ideas, that's when things fell apart. And that's when my attitude went south. My friends all had excuses. They couldn't serve together on Saturday. They couldn't support another family this Christmas. So I started casting stones at them, and to make it worse, many of those stones were thrown behind their backs. "They're just self-centered. They think that being a Christian is just about going to church on Sundays ... but it's not! They are consumeristic and selfish, and that's not how Christians are supposed to act. Why are they being so freaking lazy?!"

Whether to their face or behind their back, none of my responses helped at all. I loved my friends; they loved me, and they love Jesus, but trying to motivate them with shame and guilt didn't work. It never does. What I hadn't learned yet is how the story of God found in the Bible, which is all one big gospel story, changes everything and can rightly motivate us toward love and discipleship and mission. We are, quite literally, new creations with a new gospel identity.[1]

The good news of the gospel is not "You should or shouldn't do this or that...." Rather, because of what Jesus has done for us, on our behalf, we no longer *need* to live in certain patterns or selfish ways. Now we *get* to live in this new way of serving others and seeing all of life as an opportunity for mission.

If any of my friends from that group back in Chicago are reading this now, I am sorry.

A BETTER STORY

This understanding of our new restored identity starts in the very beginning of the Bible, in Genesis chapters 1 and 2. It is here that we first read about the main character of the story, an amazing and eternal God who always does what is good, right, and perfect. He creates this world full of life and vibrant variety, and all of it displays, in some way, God himself. That's the idea behind the word *glory* that we toss around; to see or experience the glory of God is to encounter what he is truly like.

Next we read that God creates humans, both male and female (a community) in his own three-in-one image, "to be like us."[2] Then he not only shares his authority with them by putting them in charge of the earth and all the creatures who live on it, but also sends them out with a hard-to-believe mandate: Go be fruitful and multiply; reproduce and display *my* image. Show and tell the world what I am really like and what I'm all about. It's a remarkable story and one that makes God look awesome, but it also gives great value to all human beings. In fact, God himself, at this point in the story, sits back, looks this all over, and declares the whole thing — including the humans — *very good!*[3]

Maybe you know what happens next. In Genesis 3 those first humans — our great-great-great ... great-grandparents, Adam and Eve — decide that they can manage life and the knowledge of good and evil and can judge what is right and wrong for themselves. They turn their backs on their loving Creator-Father to try and go it alone. It's as if they say to God, "I think we've got this one, Dad; we can handle life on our own. We're gonna go off and live in a way that displays *our* glory; we're gonna show the world what *we're* all about." This, in essence, is what the Bible refers to as sin. And all sin leads to death, a separation from God, the source of life.

While there is a great deal that happens after Genesis 3, I am going to skip ahead for now to the pinnacle of the gospel story. It is when God himself sends his own Son, Jesus, to rescue and restore us to a right relationship with him and our Father. Jesus, in his life, death, and resurrection, provides forgiveness for our sin and rebellion, forever puts away death, and offers us new restored identities based on who he is, not on who we are.

Then, at the end of the story we read in Revelation 21 and 22 that God himself will one day come back and live with humanity again, and all things will be restored to the way that he originally created them to be. His glory, his reality, will be on full display forever.

Pretty awesome.

One of the problems I've found is that for decades — perhaps centuries now — much of the teaching and preaching in the church emphasizes the center of the story, but it leaves off Genesis 1 and 2 and omits Revelation 21 and 22. The story typically runs from Genesis 3, where humans sin, to Revelation 20, where judgment comes. And that makes the story of

God—the entire Bible—seem focused on one thing: human sin and an inevitable punishment that awaits.[4]

The story of God does show how God deals with our sin. But it's not designed to help us with "sin management," nor is it a morality tale to teach us how to do the right stuff to please God. These are truncated and distorted versions of the story; they are man-centered instead of God-centered, focused on helping us achieve our goals instead of God's glory.

The gospel is not, "You suck and you're going to pay for it!" That does not sound like very good news.

The better story, the true, *big* gospel story is this: "You were created in the image of a loving and gracious God, destined for an eternal relationship with him. Though it is true that you have rebelled against God, thinking you could create an identity for yourself, one where you are lord over your own life, God himself came on a rescue mission to restore all people, places, and things back to relationship with him (including you), back to the way he originally designed it to be. And a day is coming when he will once again walk and live and dwell with us in a city that is like a beautiful garden forever and ever."

That is a way better story!

It is out of the full story that we understand why we were created, understand God's plans for this world, and come to know our original—and now restored—identity. Because we have God as our loving Father, we are dearly loved sons and daughters—a family. And we live as a family that has been sent and empowered by Jesus' own Spirit as missionaries, serving others as we have been served, as a way of life. We don't do this because we are supposed to, but because this is *who* we are, and we get to extend God's loving rescue mission to the ends of the earth.

We truly are a family of missionary servants sent as disciples who make disciples.

We don't live "on mission" because we are *supposed* to. It is our birthright. We *get* to do this. God loved us enough to come and die for us while we still held our fists in the air to him in defiance. He will love us no less or no more based on how *missional* we are. We love because we have been loved. We are his dearly loved children, created and restored to show the world what he is truly like.

I needed to understand and help others believe this in order to effectively motivate their (and my) hearts to live on mission with God.

A BIGGER GRACE

When you look out across your city or neighborhood and you see others in need, how do you perceive them? How do you decide who is worthy of your help? Do you only help those who find themselves, by no fault of their own, in bad situations or in great need? What about the perpetrators of crime or those who have made bad life decisions and created the mess they find themselves in? Who sits as a high priority on your "list"?

In my MC there was a single mother who consistently found herself in financial need. After getting comfortable with us, the mother (whom I'll call Cindy) grew bold enough to share her needs, and she received some help from those in our group. Over time, however, some of our folks began to grumble about helping Cindy *one more time....* They would say things such as, "If she hadn't gotten her girls those new dresses and such nice backpacks for school, she would have had the money she needs for her electric bill this month. She's using us."

Pretty icky, huh?

We had to help these weary do-gooders see that *why* our sister had come to be in great need didn't really matter all that much. If a single mom can't keep her heat and lights on, that is sad. If she is faking it to take advantage of us, that is even sadder! If anything, she *really* needs us to show her love and God's good provision. Grace works this way; it expands and grows to meet our actual sinful needs.

This is where our belief in the gospel is tested. The more needy, broken, and undeserving people are, the *more* they are (just like me and my sin) in need of grace. Jesus said that it is not the healthy who need a doctor, but the sick. He said he came not for the righteous, but for messed-up sinners.

SHAME OR SELF-RIGHTEOUSNESS

I probably could have motivated the folks in our community to continue helping this needy sister by telling them to suck it up and be "good Christians." I could have pointed out that I knew they could afford to help her if they *really wanted to*. I might have explored motivating them with, "You *should* be willing to help Cindy. After all, she's your sister, and you may need help someday yourself!" But none of this would have produced help for her out of *gospel motivation*. Whatever they did would now be motivated by one of two things: shame or self-righteousness.

Shame looks like this: "I don't know.... I guess you're right. I'm sorry. We have all been given so much in life, I really should help her with her bills." In other words, "I will feel bad (or worse) if I *don't* help her out, so I will do what you ask." Action motivated by shame shifts our focus to ourselves. It's about what I get for doing this or how I'll feel based on my action or inaction.

Self-righteousness looks like this: "Hey, Caesar, I want you to know that I did the right thing, just like you asked us to. I sent Cindy a check to help her out. Praise God, right?!" Again, our "helping" here shifts the focus back on ourselves. "Look how good I am. I did just what you asked so you'd be happy with me. I feel bad thinking that you might not be happy with me."

In both cases the motivation behind our action is self-centered. Neither shame nor self-righteousness is a good motivator for getting people to live on God's mission. Remember, God created us to show people what he is like and to be a living display of the good news we have received from him. Our gracious God is not about shaming people, and our best attempt at self-righteousness is what got us into trouble in the first place.

We don't want to model shame and self-righteous living to others. The world handles that just fine.

My buddy Hugh Halter puts it this way:

> Jesus certainly had hopes for people, and he was faithful to his personal mission, but he didn't have an agenda. He had the highest calling of any man in the world, with only three years to complete the task with barely enough people to start a volleyball team. If anyone should have had their loin cloth in a square-knot, trying to assemble the dream team, whip them

into shape, get 'em out there and get 'er done, it would have been Jesus. He should have been the most controlling, most intense, most belittling leader of all time, but he was the exact opposite and showed us how to never let goals take precedent over people.[5]

A BIGGER GOSPEL

When we understand how deeply God already loves us, not because of any performance or lack thereof on our part, but because of Jesus, it frees us to love unconditionally. We no longer love and serve others to earn anything or add to our bucket of "good feelings," but because God's love for us has already been bought and paid for. And when we know and believe the full story, understanding our true identity and seeing that we've been created and saved for a purpose, life takes on this missional aspect that I have been talking about. We begin to understand that we *exist* for God's mission. A missionary isn't just what we do; it's who we are.[6]

Jesus clarified *how* we accomplish the ultimate "why" of the gospel—the restoration of all things—by giving us his mission: *"Go and make disciples."*[7] As the arts, industry, politics, our families—all areas of culture—are increasingly filled with Jesus' disciples bringing about his gospel restoration, the earth is filled with his glory. The restoration of all things has one goal—that God would be glorified! Discipleship is the only mission that Jesus gave his church. It is how the gospel goes out and multiplies and accomplishes the restoration of all things. It is the power of the gospel that sets us free and saves us. It is the purpose of the gospel that then sends us out to make more disciples of Jesus who now live in light of the same good news.

The gospel is not just about my individual happiness or God's plan for my life. It is about God's plan for the world.

All of this requires a community to fully grasp it and live it out. It is part of God's original plan and design. Just as God himself exists in a loving, mutually submitted community, he created us to live in community with one another. We cannot fully display what God is like all by ourselves. By design, we need each other. I need constant reminders of what is now true about me because of the gospel—my gospel identity. I need others to remind me of this with their words and their lives.

UNBELIEVERS . . . ALL OF US!

Not many Christians still think of themselves as unbelievers. We normally use that term to describe people who are not Christians, people who don't claim to be disciples of Jesus. But even if you are a Christian, there are still many things about God that you actually *do not* believe. Often there is a large gap between what we *say* we believe in our head and what we truly believe in our heart. I call this our Head-Heart Distortion.

The process of closing the gap between what we know in our head and what we believe in our heart is called "sanctification." Sanctification is what discipleship is all about. I often say it this way: "Discipleship is the process of moving from unbelief to belief, concerning what is true of God, and now true of us, in every area of life." Discipleship is about becoming more like Jesus, but we will only become more like Jesus when our actions are consistent with what we say (or think) we believe.

Only the gospel can close this gap, addressing the head-heart distortion. We have well-worn grooves in our lives that need healing, mending, or a complete repaving. We need a community to walk with us, consistently loving us and reminding us of the truth.

WASHING UP

I thought Becs was going to either hit the ceiling or hit Liesel in the head with the pan she was drying off. We had just had a nice dinner with these two friends who were visiting from England. The ladies had volunteered to help with washing up in our old dishwasher-less kitchen, when Liesel said something to Becs that blew me away. They were talking about some frustration that Becs was having with an employee at work and how frustrated she was that this other person was not going along with the program.

And that's when it happened.

I heard Liesel casually say to Becs, "Hmmm, it seems that maybe your pride is being hurt. And what you're really upset about is that this person is not responding to you like you are God. Only God is great, sister; you don't have to be in control. Jesus died so you wouldn't have to be—you're free."

Becs responded with, "I do believe you're right. I don't like it when my sovereignty is thwarted . . . as if I am God over everyone else's choices. I need to repent of that. Thanks, sister!"

And off they went, finishing up the dishes and chatting away as if nothing big had happened. I stood there wondering how often they had "gospeled" each other's hearts like this. And over time I came to realize that this is *exactly* what a gospel-centered community does. That's how discipleship happens — in the flow of everyday life and activity. Even while you are washing up the dishes.

Since that time and by God's grace, we have all grown in our "gospel fluency," in our ability to speak the truth of the gospel into each other's lives. Here's another example of what this looks like, one from my own community where a younger brother "gospeled" my heart.

We were having dinner with our MC: good food, lots of laughter, kids running around everywhere. Kevin, the young leader whom I had discipled and trained to take over the leadership of our community, asked me to tell the group about an upcoming opportunity we had to serve in our city. I quickly rolled out the details of what, when, and where. Then I explained why we *should want* to all get together on Saturday for this time of serving others. I leaned pretty hard on the facts and the obvious need. I reminded our extended family that we had not been out serving much lately and how I really wanted everyone to make this a priority in their schedules.

"See you all on Saturday! Right ...?"

We finished up the evening with conversations, shared Communion together, and then hugged each other goodbye for the night. It was around nine o'clock when Tina and I went home, flipped on the TV, and started checking a few emails. Then my phone rang. It was Kevin. He asked if it would be okay if he stopped over for a few minutes. "Sure, brother, come on by!" Kevin only lived a few blocks away, so he was at our house in minutes.

He said he had a question for me about something he had noticed during our time together that evening. "Caesar, tonight when you were filling the group in on that serving thing on Saturday, where was your motivation coming from? Everyone responded positively because of who you are and their respect for you, but I was wondering about the motive. Where was the motivation for serving this weekend coming from?"

I knew that it must have been awkward and intimidating for this younger spiritual brother to approach me with a question like this. I was an elder in our church, I had trained him in leadership for years, and I was quite a bit older than him. Thankfully, instead of my getting defensive, the Spirit tapped my heart immediately. I was pretty sure I knew what Kevin was trying to point out. I asked him, "What did it feel like I was doing? How did my 'sales pitch' for this Saturday come off?"

"Well, it was just that — it seemed like you were using your influence in our group to sell us something tonight. You were nice and gentle, but the whole thing seemed like 'we *should* do this *because* . . .' instead of being motivated by the love and service we have received from Jesus. I want to remind you, bro, regardless of who shows up to serve this Saturday, you are dearly loved by the Father."

He was right.

I felt so very loved by this guy in that moment. He went on to say, "I know your heart, Caesar, and I know your true intention for our family. I just wanted to point out my observations and see what you thought." Kevin was secure in his own identity and self-worth, and he knew that God's acceptance of him was because of Jesus' service and sacrifice, and he felt free to risk approaching me with the truth in love. I thanked him for bringing this matter gently yet boldly to me. I apologized for how I had led poorly that night and asked his forgiveness, which he immediately gave me. He told me he really loved me; he hugged me and said, "Okay, thanks, brother. That's all I wanted to ask you. See you tomorrow." And he was gone.

This wasn't a big, heavy, or overly dramatic thing. The conversation happened within a couple hours of my "sales pitch" and only lasted ten to fifteen minutes. It was gentle, direct, and came in the form of a question. But it illustrates exactly what we are talking about when we think of gospel motivation and how we love others. When we risk looking bad or offending someone for the sake of sharing the gospel truth with them, we *are* loving them and Jesus more than we are loving our self in that moment. Again, even though I was being confronted in my sin, I felt very *loved* by my younger brother in the faith that evening.

The gospel is truly good news to me, and it led me to repent, turning from the motive of shame and self-righteousness. A few days later, I shared with our community what the Spirit had used Kevin to reveal to me, seeking their forgiveness too. The whole thing was simple and powerful and brought God great glory. We all learned from that experience because of the humble obedience that Kevin exhibited.

NOT THE BEST

Let me confess something else at this point. That story I shared in the last chapter about having my family eat nothing but beans and rice for dinner was *not* an example of using the gospel to motivate others. Sure, it had some positive and desired results. But can you now see the difference between gospel motivation and just getting people to do stuff that changes their outward behavior? A month spent changing your diet isn't necessarily bad. Understanding and sharing in the experiences of others can (and did) have positive effects on our lives and grow us in gratitude. But it's the *why* behind our actions that makes all the difference.

If, instead of forcing my family to participate in this experiment to shame them into changing, I had reminded them that God's grace is huge and mysterious, that Jesus died on the cross for us, showing his great love for us even while we were opposed to his rule and reign, it would have made all the difference. The fact that Jesus has given our family such undeserved blessings naturally reminds us of his love every day. Having a little less to eat for a month could have been more of a willing participation in gratefulness and a living reminder of his grace.

Outwardly, the two experiences might have looked pretty similar. But inwardly, our hearts would have pursued them for entirely different reasons. It would have been very different than just telling them, "You all complain too much and *should* be thankful!"

In fact, all of the things that we need to grow in and be willing to steward as disciples of Jesus — things that we may need to lay down for the sake of his mission — can come from fleshly and selfish motives or a gospel motivation.

Remember, the good news of the gospel is not "you should or shouldn't do this or that," but instead, because of Jesus' life, death, and resurrection, we no longer *need* to think or act in certain patterns. We *get* to live in light of what is now true of us. The gospel is truly good news for *every* area of our lives today, not just good news about the future after we die.

THE PLANK IN MY EYE

As we are learning to apply the good news of the gospel with ourselves and others, we have to be careful. Unfortunately, this can turn into something mechanical and seem as if we are quoting facts to people at their most vulnerable moments. We need to be sure that we are speaking from a place of love and seeking the other person's good and God's glory, not our own agendas, plans, or hopes for missional victories.

Gospel-motivated discipleship is a powerful thing, and when dealing with problems and with those who are unhealthy relationally or different from us, it has a way of exposing our own hearts too. My friend Tim, who lives in a gospel-centered community, said,

> When a fellow ministry leader and I faced a difficult situation, he said, "What I find most disappointing is what it has revealed about my own heart. It's shown me again that I still need people's approval, because I fear them more than I fear God." When someone is difficult, disappointing, or disrespectful, your reaction reveals your own heart. If you react with anger or bitterness, then your "need" for control or respect or success is exposed. If you're trusting God's sovereignty rather than your own abilities, and if you're concerned for God's glory rather than your own reputation, then it will be a different story.[8]

When you experience someone else's sin or unbelief, your own heart will be exposed. You may experience grace in your heart from God. But you may also discover pride and self-righteousness lurking in the dark.

I cannot emphasize enough that this all has to be a work of the Holy Spirit in our lives. We can think we are seeing things so clearly and yet be way off base, but the indwelling Spirit of God can lead, illuminate, and guide us in all the ways of truth. Remember, according to Scripture, it is the Spirit who *helps, reminds, convicts, teaches, leads, counsels,* and *reveals.* The Spirit is the true and primary discipler of people. The Spirit is the one who changes hearts and transforms lives.

> "When he [the Holy Spirit] comes, he will prove the world to be in the wrong about sin and righteousness and judgment."[9]

Practically, this means that you should *always* pray before you talk with someone, seeking wisdom from the Spirit before attempting to bring truth and love to bear in a situation. You might need to start your conversations saying, "I know I probably won't say this very well, but I want you to know I am trying to love you now, so I am going to do my best...." You want to broadcast your intentions in a humble way before diving into a conversation that may be sensitive or touchy. And timing can be everything. Just because *now* is the time you are ready to discuss something, it does not mean that it is the right time for the other person to hear it. Seek the Spirit's timing, and always look for what will best serve the other person.

Learning to understand and believe a gospel that is big enough to change the world starts with us. We need to recognize and explore the cracks and crevices in our hearts where sin and unbelief tend to hide out. This is a crucial step in living on mission and leading others. And like learning any new language, the process of developing a new gospel fluency starts small and grows slowly, but it has the power to change our families and communities, beautifully putting life in the kingdom of God on display for all who would see.

Small is Big: What is one area in your own life in which you have been try-ing to bring about change, using either shame (*If I don't do this I'm a loser!*) or self-righteousness (*I did it, so I rock!*). Ask God to remind you of his love in light of who Jesus is and what he has done for you, specifically connected to this area. This may seem like a small step, but this process of moving from unbelief to belief is at the heart of discipleship.

Slow is Fast: The patterns we use of either *shame* or *self-righteousness* are well worn with others and have often been passed on from our child-hood. Identify any ways you may be wrongly attempting to motivate others close to you and confess it to them and ask their forgiveness. Be patient with your ability to see and articulate these areas of your life with others, but begin in faith.

Multiplication Wins: It's not enough for us to learn new things and begin new practices; we must immediately begin to seed multiplication into every-thing we are learning and doing. Pick one or two people close to you whom you will now teach what you have been learning about the gospel. Perhaps it is those same people the Holy Spirit led you to confess to regarding your attempted motivations with them, using shame or self-righteousness. Teach them *why* you are doing this as well.

Signpost: At this point in the journey you have begun the real quest: to know and believe the *whole* gospel story and apply it to your life and others. This is at the very center of discipleship. Gospel fluency and the under-standing of your true transformed identity are something of great value and you must never stop growing in them and leading others in faith. The gospel is not the beginning of the journey as a Christian; it is good news for *all* of life!

CHAPTER 4

SAINTS AND SINNERS

"What a view!" The food was good, the wine was decent, and the place was starting to fill up. My wife and I were killing a few hours on the boardwalk of the Jersey Shore and had grabbed a bite to eat while doing some people watching. Just as we had started sipping our second glass of wine and diving into some of the best fried calamari we'd ever eaten, a couple of women sat down a few seats from us, just around the corner of the bar. We later learned that Eileen and her nearly eighty-year-old mother were regulars at this place.

Our conversation began when I leaned over to Eileen's mom and jokingly said, "I don't want you to think me forward or fresh, and I am here with my wife today, but I must say that you have the most *beautiful* blue eyes!" She lit up with a smile and a twinkle in her eye and said, "I wish you *were* getting fresh!" I think she blushed a little. We all laughed, introduced ourselves, and exchanged a few comments about how the weather was starting to change. Then we went back to our own conversations for a few minutes.

Tina and I laughed, thinking that these women were pretty fun and easy to talk to. I could overhear them debating what they were going to eat for lunch that day. They agreed that they were *not* going to have the calamari, one of their favorites; instead they were going to try something else on the menu this week. They ordered a salad and a plate of potato skins to share, still wondering if they had made a mistake by not ordering the calamari.

Tina and I looked at each other and had the same thought at that moment. We called our server over and asked him to order a plate of the delicious calamari for our new friends and put it on our tab. Eileen and her mom were a little ways into their gin and tonics when their salad and potato skins arrived, and then a few minutes later the surprise dish showed up. They let the waiter know that it wasn't theirs. "We *love* these things, but we did not order the calamari this week; there must be some mistake." The waiter informed them that we had, in fact, sent them over as a gift. The women turned to see us grinning ear-to-ear, and raising our glasses in a toast, we said, "To the calamari! Enjoy them on us."

That's when the afternoon went from good to great.

For the next thirty or forty minutes we enjoyed our food and drinks together. The conversation went places that you could not imagine as we found topic after topic that we shared in common. Soon others at the bar were looped in and had sent food over to us! We were sad when we had to leave. But before doing so, we exchanged numbers with Eileen and made a promise to get together for a meal at a fancy French culinary school in New York in a few weeks when our schedules lined up.

A week later, while teaching in another city, I called Eileen to say hello and let her know that we were still traveling but had not forgotten about them and our afternoon on the shore. She said, "My mom and I were just talking about you guys! That was absolutely *the best time* we have ever had. I am not kidding. We have gone to that place for decades and never had so much fun. We can't wait to see you and Tina." A short time later she called my cell phone to settle on a date for our promised dinner, saying that they had met another lady at the same bar/café and told her all about us and that she was now going to join us for dinner, promising we would love her too.

It's amazing, isn't it? We often find ourselves thinking how easy and fun it is to do this stuff. I mean, really! We're not all that great or anything. We spent very little time with these lovely ladies, dropped a few dollars on an appetizer for them, and mostly *listened*. And it was "the best time" they ever had! We know that God arranged and blessed that unplanned encounter, but it leads me to wonder how many (many, many) more of these types of opportunities and how many more people are out there waiting to be loved on, listened to, and scooped into the Family by God's kids.

But you gotta be out there to find them.

GOD HAS A FAMILY

As we began to unpack in the last chapter, God's plan to redeem and restore all people and places has always been wrapped up in his desire to have a family that he would do this with and through. Paraphrasing Exodus 19:3–6:

> God called down to Moses from the mountain saying, Tell the people of Israel: "You saw what I did to Egypt and how I carried you on eagles' wings and brought you out of slavery, back to me. If you will obey me and keep my covenant, out of all peoples you will be my own special treasure. The whole Earth is mine to choose from, but you are special: a kingdom of priests, a holy nation set apart to represent me."

A special people, set apart to represent God to the rest of the world. That's how God wanted Israel to live, but they refused. Instead, they turned inward and treated those who were different from them as "outsiders," people to be avoided (or maybe tolerated) instead of embraced.

So when Jesus, God with flesh on, shows up on the planet, he is accused of all sorts of evil by the religious elite of the day. And he makes friends with lots of different people — people those elite don't like, people on the outside. Jesus invites them to the party, to the table, and to walk in his ways.

Then, after his death and resurrection Jesus sent his Holy Spirit to dwell inside his disciples — other humans. They would now be the flesh that was wrapped around his Spirit, out accomplishing the Father's mission. The apostle Paul called this whole amazing development "the mystery revealed" (see, for example, Ephesians 3:3–6). God himself would now dwell among and inside his people, and they would be his body throughout the world. Here's the catch: people are not looking for doctrine. They're looking for a God with skin on, whom they can know, speak with, learn from, struggle with, be honest with, get straight answers from, and connect their lives to.[1]

This is why we must go. This is why we cannot be content with our convenient circle of friends and those most like us. We go because that's how God is, and we exist to show the world what our Dad is like.

FRIEND OF SINNERS

Far too often I have heard Christians say, somewhat sheepishly but with a hint of self-righteousness, that they really have nothing in common with non-Christians. That's why they don't have many (or any) not-yet-believing friends. Or they tell me that they don't hang out with *lost* people, or allow their kids to, because they are trying to remain "holy" and don't want to become polluted by the world. And to those objections I almost want to laugh and ask them if they have ever really read their Bibles or looked in a mirror.

First off, Scripture and virtually all of history have shown us that if there is one thing we have *most* in common with every other human being, it's our sinful nature. Yet usually we let others' sins define them and divide us, when in fact we are all sinners in need of a savior. We're all dying, literally, and in need of rescue. We're just alike.

And as for the idea that we should avoid people to remain holy—come on! Jesus was the holiest person who ever walked on this planet. In fact, his holiness—the way he perfectly imaged the character and nature of God—is what led him to hang out with people whom the religious establishment had declared unclean. Our ongoing involvement and relationship with others, especially those on the margins, begins when we profoundly grasp God's grace. Our selfish and fearful instincts are to keep our distance. But Jesus let people like that kiss his feet. He's the friend of riffraff, traitors, the unrespectable, drunks, druggies, prostitutes, the mentally ill, the broken, and the needy—people whose lives are a mess. He ate with them, hung out with them, and invited them on a journey.[2]

> The Son of Man came eating and drinking, and they say, "Here is a glutton and a drunkard, a friend of tax collectors and sinners."[3]

If you were to honestly look at your life, your church, or maybe even the denomination you are a part of, could anyone ever bring this same accusation against you? Are you a friend of sinners?

Some people respond to this Matthew 11:19 verse saying, "No! Jesus is not a friend to sinners, only to those who obey him." And they cite John 15:14 as their justification. What a horrible example of proof-texting! The entire passage there has Jesus explaining how he loved his disciples and chose them while they were still jacked up and far from God. Can you imagine a parent saying that to their kids? "You are only my child when you obey me. Otherwise I don't love you." What? That would be crazy. And it is. That is the exact *opposite* of the heart of our Father and his Son, Jesus.

TWO SIDES OF THE SAME COIN

But there is more. It's not just that Jesus befriended and blessed sinful people. Rather, we see that they liked him back and accepted him and treated him as their friend. In Luke 7 we see Jesus at a meal in the home of a Pharisee, a powerful religious leader in those days.

> A woman in that town who lived a sinful life learned that Jesus was eating at the Pharisee's house, so she came there with an alabaster jar of perfume. As she stood behind him at his feet

weeping, she began to wet his feet with her tears. Then she
wiped them with her hair, kissed them and poured perfume
on them.[4]

Notice that because of Jesus' reputation in the community,
this woman comes to him, risking the scorn of the Pharisee.
She then treats Jesus with a shocking degree of intimacy. It is
not considered appropriate behavior when she lets down her
hair to wipe her tears from Jesus' feet.[5] She clearly loves Jesus
and feels certain that he will accept her and not send her
away. The narrative concludes with Jesus forgiving her of her
sins and commending her for her faith. Many scholars believe
that this same woman is Mary Magdalene, who would become
one of Jesus' closest friends and followers during his ministry.

Are we, like Jesus, seen as people of grace and acceptance? Do
others feel safe to approach you, even with their sins and screw-
ups? Would you be willing to be a friend with a person regardless of whether they share your beliefs or join your cause?

> "I've told you these things for a purpose: that my joy might
> be your joy, and your joy wholly mature. This is my com-
> mand: Love one another the way I loved you. This is the very
> best way to love. Put your life on the line for your friends.
> You are my friends when you do the things I command you.
> I'm no longer calling you servants because servants don't
> understand what their master is thinking and planning. No,
> I've named you friends because I've let you in on everything
> I've heard from the Father."[6]

Here Jesus is saying to his disciples, "I've been a friend to you
(even before you really got it or knew who I was). Now you'll
be a good friend back to me if you go out and do what I did
and what I am calling you to do: go be a friend to similar outsiders, and disciple them to know and trust me."

Jesus said that those who walk in his ways and live as his disciples will come to know the truth that sets them free.[7] Are we willing to invite others to walk with us in the everyday stuff of life as we, *together*, learn to do good in the ways of Jesus? Do we believe that our own sanctification and the daily working out of our salvation will be alongside the unlovable?

PUB PASTOR

When we first moved to Tacoma, Tina and I worked hard to figure out the rhythms of the city and our neighborhood in particular. Where did people eat? What parks did they regularly spend time in? Where did they go for fun? A big part of the culture in Tacoma is eating and hanging out at pubs or bars. They are a favorite place to go, see your friends, and make new ones. And since many of our new neighbors and half the city seemed to frequent the pubs, we figured that we had better pick a few regular places and start hanging out there at least two or three times a week. We learned that not only were pubs and bars a great place to meet new people, but they were the perfect place to run into others that we had met elsewhere. We saw neighbors, coworkers, the folks at the tattoo shop, the young lady who works at the grocery store—all of them were at the pubs too. As we got to know the names of the people working in these places, they began to remember our names as well and would introduce us to other regular patrons and friends of theirs.

All of this was actually quite easy. All we really had to do was be nice to people, ask good questions, listen to their stories, buy a round once in a while, and be a *great* tipper. If you do these five simple things, everyone will remember you and will be excited to see you.

As we did this in a regular rhythm over time, I started to be affectionately referred to as the "pub pastor." In fact, a group of twentysomethings known as the Tacoma Party Crew made me their chaplain, so to speak, and they made my wife the official TPC Mom. This bunch, who were friends with our own kids, started hanging out at our house for more and more meals as we talked and laughed and became a family.

Through building relationships this way and being the unofficial pub pastor to a diverse group of friends and acquaintances, I have had the opportunity to counsel with people, perform weddings and funerals, pray with and for many, help people financially, teach them to cook, show them how to set up a household budget ... you name it. We've had the opportunity to be a blessing because we pressed into the rhythms of our culture and treated people, not as targets or goals, but the way we wanted to be treated: as friends and family.

In a sense, what we have been doing is "re-parenting" the culture. It wasn't that these friends didn't have parents, but in our relationships we were inviting them to taste and see what life is like in the family of God. We tried to show them what it's like to be in a family that has God as their dad and Jesus as their brother.

By simply hanging out and having an open home, we developed hundreds of relationships with folks at all stages of their spiritual journey in Tacoma ... and around the world. It was quite a contrast to my life in Chicago. Remember that in those days I didn't have a single non-Christian, not-yet-believing friend. But now God's love and grace were motivating our hearts and the Spirit was leading us to live with much greater gospel-intentionality.

Recently Tina and I moved to Manhattan to help others learn to live in community on mission. So where do you think we started as we tried to make new friends? Yep, we went to the pubs. We hosted a "happy hour" in our small apartment on Wednesday nights, inviting folks from our building and neighborhood to join us for appetizers and drinks. What a blast!

WHO'S IN, WHO'S OUT?

When I was growing up, whether it was hanging around my neighborhood or on the school playground, or spending time with my siblings and cousins during family celebrations, it was important to feel as if I was one of the *cool kids*—one of the *insiders*. No one likes to feel on the outs or be pushed to the margins of the social circle.

We all want to be insiders.

Jesus is the *ultimate* insider; he is God! And yet he came and lived like an outsider. He grew a beard and took on a scratchy robe and handmade sandals of his culture to be with sinners and outcasts. To hang out with the *un-cool* kids. And then he took the sin of these outsiders and put it upon himself on the cross. He traded his perfect life for their messed-up, broken, and rebellious lives, treating them like *insiders* in the kingdom of God.

We are all outsiders.

Created in the image of our divine God, we have all chosen a life outside of God's will, outside of his love and protection, because of our sin and rebellion. But Jesus came and changed the rules on the playground, loving the unlovable outsiders, offering grace and forgiveness.[8]

He accepted us and willingly took our sins upon himself, and that's why we willingly now go and accept and serve others. We shoulder the sins of others by taking up their pain and sharing their burdens. We invite them to the party. We spend time loving the unlovable of the world because we have been loved by Jesus.[9]

THE POWER OF 21

You've heard me mention all of the meals and parties we regularly have as a family and a community. Why do we do this? It's all part of this same kingdom trajectory we saw Jesus engage in with his disciples and the people he encountered throughout his life. Meals come around in natural rhythm for everyone, every day, providing ample opportunities for discipleship and mission. Case in point, did you realize that there are three ways the New Testament completes the sentence, "The Son of Man came …"?

> "The Son of Man came *not to be served but to serve*, and to give his life as a ransom for many."[10]
>> "The Son of Man came *to seek and to save the lost*."[11]
>> "The Son of Man came *eating and drinking* …"[12]

The first two are statements of purpose. Why did Jesus come? He came to serve, to give his life as a ransom, to seek and save the lost. But the third statement identifies Jesus' method. How did Jesus come, serving and seeking and saving the lost? He came eating and drinking.

Jesus was a party animal. His mission strategy was a long meal, stretching into the evening. He discipled people around a table with some grilled fish, a loaf of bread, and a pitcher of wine.

Just looking at Luke's gospel, we find story after story of Jesus eating with people. He eats with tax collectors and sinners at the home of Levi,[13] and as already mentioned, he is anointed by Mary with oil at the home of Simon the Pharisee during a meal.[14] We see Jesus teaching kingdom principles and pulling off great feasts when he feeds the multitudes,[15] but he also spends an evening with just a few close friends sharing a meal with two sisters named Martha and Mary.[16] He hammers the hypocrisy of the Pharisees and teachers of the Law during a meal.[17] It is while eating that Jesus encourages people to invite the poor to their meals, rather than always inviting friends.[18] Jesus invites himself to dinner with Zacchaeus[19] and shares his last evening before the cross with his disciples over a meal.[20] Then after his resurrection, Jesus has a meal with two of his disciples in Emmaus and later eats a simple meal of boiled fish with the disciples in Jerusalem.[21]

Meals offer us one of the easiest opportunities to disciple others and share God's love. Most of us are *already* eating three meals a day, seven days a week. That gives us twenty-one chances to casually yet effectively share life and God's kingdom without feeling the pressure to add something new to our schedule.

It's just a matter of intentionality.

PEOPLE OF PEACE

Let's assume I have sold you on the value of having meals with people as part of your discipleship strategy, following in the footsteps of Jesus. But you might still be wondering, "Okay, who exactly do I start having these meals with?" Let's look at what Jesus told his disciples when he sent them out on mission.

The Lord now chose seventy-two other disciples and sent them ahead in pairs to all the towns and places he planned to visit. These were his instructions to them.... "Whenever you enter someone's home, first say, 'May God's peace be on this house.' If those who live there are peaceful, the blessing will stand; if they are not, the blessing will return to you. Don't move around from home to home. Stay in one place, eating and drinking what they provide. Don't hesitate to accept hospitality, because those who work deserve their pay.

"Heal the sick, and tell them, 'The Kingdom of God is near you now.'"[22]

So Jesus sends his disciples out looking for People of Peace — those who would be initially open to them, to him, and to the good news of the kingdom. Notice that Jesus sent them out in pairs as part of a larger team. This life of discipleship, which includes finding people of peace, is not a solo endeavor. Do this with another friend or couple. Next, Jesus tells them to pronounce a blessing of peace over folks who invite them into their lives. This doesn't have to be a literal pronouncement: "May God's peace be on your house!" People would be like, "What?!" The idea here is that you are to be a blessing and see who blesses you back.

Jesus also says to stick with those people, not to jump around from house to house, group to group, but to hang out with the people who are open to you. In other words, who are the people in your life that are *leaning in* to relationship and faith? We all have them. They are friends, coworkers, neighbors, or extended family members who just sort of ... like us. They know we are Christians, and they're not freaked out by it. In fact, they might be a little curious. Who is like that in your life right now?

It may be that a potential Person of Peace is one of your children's friends, those kids who love hanging around your house or are always inviting your kids over to play. They may be the gatekeeper to their entire family and a whole host of new relationships. Here's a great summary of what it takes to get started in this from my pal Ben Sternke:

1. Find the Person of Peace — the person who is open to you, is interested in you, likes you, wants to be around you.

2. Go to *their* turf, where they're comfortable.

3. Allow them to serve you or show you hospitality.

4. Spend intentional time with them, and . . .

5. Be ready to do the works of the kingdom and speak the good news of the kingdom (in appropriate ways).[23]

WHO'S YOUR ONE?

On many occasions I have had people say to me, "I'm not this huge gatherer and people person. I'm not naturally wired as the life of the party."

I tell them not to worry. The more naturally gifted, Type A, super-outgoing folks in your community will put you into proximity with lots of people. Just be nice and look for the *one* who is leaning in to relationship, that certain person whom you easily click with. God will guide others to specific and unique fits in relationship with the rest.

Don't miss this "small is big" insight: Who's your one?

In the parable of the lost sheep,[24] Jesus tells about a huge flock of one hundred beloved sheep and a shepherd who goes out searching for that *one* sheep that slipped away. The shepherd loves all the sheep, but he is moved to search for one specific lost sheep.

So who's your one? Ask the Holy Spirit to point out that person to you right now. Chances are you already know this person. When you have an individual in mind, ask the Spirit, "What next? What is the next small step that you want me to take with this person?" Then be obedient to what you have heard and move slowly forward with another "What next, Lord?" as your relationship develops.

Imagine what might happen if you and a few other Christian friends all identified just one or two people like this and began to intentionally reorganize and prioritize your life around these people of peace. And then imagine what might happen if you made sure to include them in more and more of the rhythm of your collective lives.

That's what I'm talking about!

GO FOR FIT

I went bowling with my brother-in-law the other night. He's not much of a bowler, but he sure is a lot of fun to watch. I've noticed that everyone, whether they're good or bad at this sport, has their own little nuance when they bowl. Each person has some funny little step or slide to their delivery, a wiggle or a shake. Some folks lean hard to one side and try to wave the ball over to hit the pins. Everybody sort of figures out what works best for them.

When you are trying to figure out where your playground is, where you are going to focus your energy on mission, and where your people of peace are to be found, be sure to make it fit naturally into your stage of life and personality. You are who God made you, and he has specific people he wants you to help bring into his family.

I have a friend in Los Angeles who is an amazing mother of three kids and who, through tears, told me how she had such a hard time trying to hang out late at night in bars and clubs in LA. She felt guilty because she was not able to be out with her unbelieving friends as often as she had hoped, discipling and doing life with them. Keep in mind that she is a thirty-something mom. The late-night bar scene is probably not her tribe at all. She isn't going to be the Pub Pastor!

But she can open her heart and home to be the place where her friends bring those new friends for a meal, a safe place to hang out, a couch to crash on. She certainly has her part in the kingdom and her missional community, but as a mother with three young kids, it's probably not going to be out in the bars very often.

GETTING STARTED

What are the environments in your life right now that you can intentionally frequent to build relationships and look for that one person (or people) of peace whom God wants you to meet? Chances are that some of these things are already a part of your normal everyday life, but here are a few ideas to get you started:

- Your neighborhood

- Where you work

- Gym/CrossFit/sporting activity (e.g., biking, running)

- At the park with your kids or their sports teams

- Kids' schools (volunteer as a room mom or teacher's helper)

- Local café, pub, restaurants

- Breakfast clubs (host a brunch or open house once a month)

- "Happy hours" at your home

- Progressive dinners (invite friends to each host one course of a five-or-six-course meal, moving from house to house)

- Weekly BBQs or cookouts in your (or others') yard

Shortly after moving to New York, I started to keep a list on my smartphone of everyone I met whom I thought I might run into again: folks in my building, new friends, bartenders and staff at pubs, businesspeople I had met. I needed a way to prop up my bad memory for when I ran into them again, and I wanted to regularly pray for each of them, asking God, "What's next?"

GETTING STUCK

I realize that we are all busy and it is easy to lose focus and a sense of intentionality. New habits and rhythms take time to develop. Here are some of the common sticking points and objections I regularly hear — all of them heart issues — that can get in the way of building relationships for the kingdom:

- Adding things to "my" schedule; time issues

- Love of self/fear of rejection/perception as being "uncool"

- No one wants religion "jammed down their throat"

- Perceived cultural barriers

- "This won't work here, because ..." (too urban, too sub-urban, too busy, too scared, too diverse, too young ...)

- "I have too many friends already ..."

- "I don't know how to talk to people about God"—gospel fluency issues. We don't know how to talk to people about Jesus. We keep our mouths closed because we are afraid.[25]

IT'S A LOVE THING

When we only hang out with our own families or other Christians all the time, we not only are committing the sin of Israel and their isolation from others, but are living out a dead-end spiral of self-fulfilling prophecy. "Oh, nobody is interested in anything to do with church or Jesus or anything...."

We gotta get out there!

As Ben Sternke puts it,

> If you love Jesus, and you love people, you're going to want to be out there where the action is. If you find yourself distracted by everything, uninterested or feeling jaded about helping people get to know Jesus, you may be suffering from a lack of love. Either a lack of love for people; you're more worried about your pride and appearance, or a lack of love for Jesus; you really don't think he's all that great.[26]

But if you really grasp the degree to which God loves you and believe that the gospel is really good news for everyone, you will let those fears and old patterns of self-love fall away.

Give them to Jesus. He's *your* friend too.

Small is Big: How do you currently make new friends? Identify one or two places or activities you can engage in to regularly hang out and build new relationships. Start moving from an event-to-event mentality toward looking for things you can begin to do in rhythm with others ... over and over.

Slow is Fast: Who's your "one"? Begin to invite just one not-yet-believing friend or couple over for dinner *each* week. Don't rush to "get them saved"; take your time, and be a good friend and listener. Remember that the mission is to make disciples.

Multiplication Wins: Who is another Christian friend or couple you could invite over for dinner as well to begin to cross-pollinate these two relationships? What other normal life activity can you begin to have others join you in instead of going it alone? Do it!

Signpost: Relationships are the currency of the kingdom. Now you are looking to expand the circles and rhythms of your life to build relationships with those who could be a part of your growing missional community. Trust God for those people he wants you to be discipled by and those he is asking you to disciple. This is a "skill set" that you must learn and reproduce effectively in others to see multiplication and movement happen.

CHAPTER 5

INTO THE FRAY

I am not much of a sports guy and never really have been. I tried my hand at various sports as a kid and while in middle and high school, but alas, I had neither the genes nor the ambition to be very good or supercompetitive at sports. My son, on the other hand, is more of a natural athlete—especially when compared to me. He did pretty well in soccer and rugby, but when I asked him what he enjoyed most about playing, his answer surprised me. He said that his favorite part was just *being on the team*. Like his father, what he loved most was hanging out, being a part of something bigger than himself, enjoying that bond that comes from sharing goals and experiences with others.

When my kids were young, there were times when they treated each other in ways that were the exact opposite of this. They acted as if they were on opposing teams, and they would do whatever it took to see the other team lose and be punished for it. As parents, Tina and I felt we had to do something to help our kids get on the same page and on the same team. This was especially important when I traveled for extensive periods of time. I needed the children to be a cohesive and loving unit that pulled together, helped out their mom, helped each other, and lived as if they actually cared for one another.

Team K was born.

Tina and I came up with a way to implant all of this into the heads and hearts of our little band of *Kalinowskis*. We told the kids they were a part of something amazing, something important, and that we needed them to understand this and live more like a *team*. We even took them to the mall and had some really cheesy aqua-colored T-shirts airbrushed with the words *"Team K"* on the front. Yes, a matching shirt for each of us in our own size. And we would all wear them occasionally at the dinner table or when it was time to do yard work or serve a neighbor or someone else in the community. "Come on, kids, Team K time! We're going out to shovel snow for Mrs. Smith!" Or "When I'm out of town for the next few weeks, I really hope that Team K will be super helpful around the house, praying for each other and being a big help to Mom."

As corny as all of this sounds, it worked. "Team K" became the thing we used to identify our family at its best, a rallying cry to serve others and hang out together. Others began to refer to our family by this moniker also. Many still do.

I know, right now you're wishing that you could be a part of Team K too.

It wasn't long before this team spirit was something our friends (and their friends) coveted, getting invited to a family dinner night with Team K. We always had lots of food, laughter, and encouragement to spread around, and you knew everyone was happy that *you* were there. There was always an extra place at the table. These mealtimes, along with our other Team K adventures, were the beginning of a way of life for us — a way of sharing and extending the blessings and grace that God had poured out onto our family.

Our family life was expanding into our community. Our family life was extending *Jesus'* family life.

A FAMILY ON MISSION

Like our Master, Jesus, we must lead with our lives, not just our words. Our own family on mission is at the center of everything we do, who we are, and what we build. We will never lead another group of friends or anyone else farther and deeper into discipleship and mission than our own family. Missional communities are just an extension of our own family life patterns and mission. I don't say this because it is a new idea or a pragmatic way of looking at discipleship or evangelism — this is, in fact, how the original *church* functioned.

In the New Testament the Greek word *oikos* is used to refer to "households" — which were, in essence, extended families that functioned together with a common purpose and mission. To get a sense of this, think of your immediate family along with the circle of people who make up your closest, most important relationships: your close friends, maybe some cousins or aunts and uncles, and perhaps your neighbors or the people you work with who are really fond of you and hang with you all the time. These are the people with whom you are regularly, intentionally "doing life" together.

In the early church, discipleship and mission always centered around and flourished in the *oikos*.[1] It was these extended households that then multiplied as they sent "family members" to other parts of the city or world to embody and preach the good news of the kingdom of God. The *oikos* is the most historically common way to understand the functioning of the early church. Unfortunately—and this is especially true of recent Western culture—we've lost this sense of extended families joining together on mission. Church, for most of us, has become a building or an event that we attend once or twice a week. Our faith has become "personal" and private, mirroring our fragmented family life where we live primarily as individuals and nuclear families. But this is not healthy, nor is it biblical.

The rampant individualism of Western culture has severely damaged our society, *and* it has limited our understanding of the essence and function of the church around the world. People are now more lonely and depressed than ever as they struggle to balance careers with raising kids, all while trying to find meaning and purpose in life—without a community to surround and support them.

However, as Christians who are filled with Jesus' own spirit, we have an amazing opportunity and privilege to reshape our culture by living as God's own "extended family," a family that is built not on bloodlines or ancestry, but on Jesus. Our goal is not to have a group or program that we call our "missional community." Our co-mission is to lovingly invite the people God has purposely brought into our lives to join us in community as together we share the story of the gospel, make disciples, and learn to live as an extended family following Jesus together.

That's what starting a missional community is really all about. This is not a fad or the latest church growth technique or a new name for small groups or cell groups. It is rediscovering the church as *oikos*—an extended family on mission—where everyone is important and has a vital role to play.[2]

I like to think of it this way: Joining God on his mission is joining his family. It's going with our Dad and Brother Jesus, guided and empowered by the Holy Spirit, out into the world to do the family business.

HE'S WAY AHEAD OF YOU

At this point what you're really starting to do is bring some intentionality to this idea of identifying the people of peace in your life and beginning to live together like an extended family. The thing about the people of peace strategy is that it's not simply practical. That is, it's not just a convenient way to find people to disciple. It's actually a way of noticing what God is already doing in your mission context. Here's why: a Person of Peace isn't just someone who likes you.

Jesus told us, "Whoever listens to you listens to me,"[3] so if we are representing Jesus, these people are actually showing us that they are interested in him! They are people in whom God has already been working, preparing their hearts for the good news of Jesus. So we "stay with them" because in doing so, we aren't working alone. We are joining in with what God is doing in their lives, cooperating with the Holy Spirit.[4]

> *"Finding a Person of Peace means discovering where God is already at work in the neighborhood or network of relationships you're seeking to reach."*
>
> —MIKE BREEN

ASK AND OBEY

All of this is not just about building relationships and hanging out with people. If we are not careful, we can end up being the nicest, friendliest people in the neighborhood but fail to lead anyone one step closer to walking in the ways of Jesus. It's easy to get distracted and forget about the mission we've been sent on: go and make disciples.

So how do we naturally, in ways that don't freak people out or make us feel stupid, move into relationships that are more like the *oikos* we've learned about from Scripture—families who are helping people walk in the ways of Jesus so that they will come to know the truth that sets them free?[5]

Let me share with you a simple process that I've come to call "What next, Lord?" Not too long ago, Tina and I joined a few other friends who wanted to move beyond their weekly Bible study experience into living more like a family of missionaries.

We started out by having weekly barbecues together. One couple would host one week, and another the next. We went back and forth like this for several weeks. We handed out homemade flyers, inviting people to come for a casual meal to "get to know their neighbors." Over time, as is always the case, we noticed some natural relationships developing with some of these new friends who were coming back every week.

Tina quickly hit it off with a gal who grew up in the same city she did. I was becoming fast friends with a guy who also played guitar and loved riding motorcycles—Harleys, to be specific. We found that while we didn't all instantly become super close with everyone who came to our dinners, some people were definitely leaning in to relationship. One of the women worked in the same field as Sarah, a leader in our MC, and they hit it off. That's how it went. Each of us naturally built friendships with one or two others. It seemed that God was giving us specific relational favor with a few.

We began to pray for these relationships, asking, "What next, Lord? What do you want us to do next, *specifically*, with each of these people you have brought into our lives?" We all felt that the Spirit spoke directly to our hearts the things we were to do next to develop these relationships and love our friends. It wasn't anything profound or crazy; it was stuff like, "Give Christy a call this week to see how that job interview went that she was nervous about." Or "Call Mike and see if he can pick you up from the airport when you return later this week." We shared what we believed we had heard from God and agreed to pray for one another that week — both for favor and that we would be obedient to our "What next?" opportunities.

We got together weekly to share how we each had followed through the previous week. Then we would pray again, "What next, Lord?" God did amazing things over the next several weeks. It seemed as if we were being divinely guided into "perfect" conversations and situations with these neighbors. I think we were. Our hope, and what we had asked God to guide us into relationally, was the opportunity to take some of our neighbors through the Story-formed Way, which is a means of introducing people to the full storyline of the Bible in community in a really cool way.[6]

The group ended up inviting seven of these people to join us for this time together over the next ten weeks, and six of them agreed. The one gal who wasn't ready to do that with us remained close to our circle of friends. It wasn't as if we rejected her because she said no. She stayed part of our community, and we love her. We still hope and pray for her to "lean in" to a deeper relationship with us and with Jesus, but for now she is where she is.

We saw God do some great things over the next weeks and months together with this group, and we fell deeply in love with our new friends. God used his story and our lives together in community to help several come to faith in him as they began to walk in his ways together with us. We continue to pray for them, and for us,

"What next, Lord?"[7]

A process like this involves being together intentionally with those whom you have identified as People of Peace, some of *their* friends, and those whom you're still trying to figure out as to where they're at and whether they may be leaning in to relationship. It is both intentional and spontaneous, allowing the Holy Spirit to guide you and the MC. This is how things move from just being about you and your family to becoming a functioning *oikos* or extended family on mission.

ORGANIZED AND ORGANIC

I have found it helpful to think about life in an MC through two filters: *organized* and *organic*. In the same way that natural, healthy family life contains both of these elements, some aspects of life together are "organized" and structured, and some aspects are more "organic" or natural. We will need to nurture our extended families in both the organized and organic parts of life in community. Some of us fall into the more "organized" side of life in community; years in "small groups" may have taught us this. "See ya next week at our missional community ..." can unwittingly become our replacement for "See ya next week at church!" if we are not mindful of the natural rhythms that life as a family should and can take on.

Think for a moment about your immediate family or a group of friends. You probably don't think about that time you spend with them as a succession of events you need to attend (or worse, something you might skip if you're too busy). We don't generally tell our friends, "We already met once this week; why do we need to get together again?" They are our friends. We enjoy getting together. We don't think of our time together as one more night out or as some kind of obligation we need to fulfill. And when we think about our families, we don't count up the number of events per week that we attend with them. We live with them! There is a fabric to our life together that cannot be reduced to a series of "events."[8]

This doesn't mean that events and planned activities aren't good or necessary. A healthy family life does include planned-out events and reoccurring activity, but we don't see these as something separate and distinct, because it's all mixed into the normal rhythm and flow of our life together. Things like bedtimes, meals, homework, and chores often do take place in an organized way. These are important, and they need to get done, so we put them on a calendar of some sort, and they come around time and again. But we don't see these things as the sum total of our life together as a family.

This week, while I am writing this chapter, my family is together celebrating Thanksgiving. There are definitely parts of this holiday that we plan out. In fact, we almost follow a script in preparing our favorite Polish foods cooked "just like Grandma used to make," or in using the old pink platters made out of indestructible melamine[9] that we *must* use as plates for the meal, or watching a favorite holiday movie and several football games on television. You probably have similar organized aspects, traditions, and reoccurring things you do during the holidays as well.

These activities provide continuity, and they hold great value for us. But those organized things we do together are accentuated and enlivened by the myriad spontaneous interactions and stuff we do in between—the jokes told and conversations had while cooking together or watching the game, while on a walk to the neighborhood store, a trip in the evening to a favorite pub, or a last stroll in the park to look at the lights. Often, just the hours spent on the couch under blankets watching nothing in particular on TV become cherished and important aspects of our time together. Life happens in these unplanned, ordinary moments. Ideas and dreams are shared, correction and forgiveness are extended, and our bonds as a family are renewed and strengthened.

So life as a family is both organized and organic. We have our more organized and planned-out elements, but we also have plenty of time to just "hang out and be" as well. How weird it would be if one of our family members or close friends showed up only for the meal and left immediately afterward since there were no more "planned activities." Or if one of my kids decided to skip our massive and cherished Thanksgiving feast because they were tired or just didn't feel like coming. It wouldn't feel right. I know that sometimes things like that *do* happen within a family dynamic, but a healthy family includes commitments to one another in both the structured *and* the more spontaneous elements of life together.[10]

Think of it as being like a piece of cross-stitch artwork. The initial fabric with the pattern on it provides the framework and structure; the colorful stitches and needlework you add to that bring the whole thing to life. Without the regularity of the pattern, you would have nothing, and the stitch work would be random and meaningless. On the other hand, no one hangs up a white canvas cross-stitch pattern with a black-and-white outline on it. The true beauty comes when the different colors and textures are added in.

My friend Mike Breen puts it quite strongly when he says, "If your missional community is only doing organized events, it will fail. If your missional community is only committed to the organic 'hanging out' together, it will fail."[11]

I would encourage you to reflect on your own natural tendencies in all of this. Are you more naturally structured, or are you spontaneous? Depending on your personality, your upbringing, and even your unique spiritual gifts, you probably lean more to one side of this spectrum than the other. But a healthy MC needs both, so you will need to learn how to function and grow within both dynamics. If you need to use a calendar to schedule your regular, organized interactions, then do so; we all plan out things that are important to us. To enhance the organic aspects of life in my own MC, we began using a simple online SMS text messaging aggregator[12] so that we could easily, on the spur of the moment, let everyone know pretty much anything we were going out to do and invite anyone to join in.

There are some things that are typically more organized in missional community life:

- Weekly dinners together

- All-community serving activities

- Times of studying the Bible or going through the Story of God

- Regular prayer for the People of Peace in your life ("What next, Lord?")

- An evening just for the ladies, or a guys' night out

Pretty much anything that includes the entire community or is reoccurring will need to be organized or it probably won't last very long or be very well run.

There are also things that are more organic in missional community life:

- A few of you getting together to watch a game or see a movie

- Last-minute dinners or drinks together

- Yard work or house projects such as painting or spring cleaning

- Conversations that happen along the way

- Prayer for needs and issues that arise

Don't shy away from calling those who say they want to be a part of your MC to a high level of commitment to both the organized and organic elements of life together. All of this is part of truly feeling like an extended family. Remember, we exist to show others what life in our Father's family is really all about.

Healthy families are both organized and organic.

BEGIN AT THE BEGINNING

Think *small is big* and *slow is fast* for a moment. I want to suggest that you initially try to have at least three touch points of interaction per week as a community. Along with some of the others from your extended missional family, try to see each other or be together a few times around the following organized or planned-out experiences: a family dinner, a DNA group or Huddle,[13] and your current or evolving church's Sunday gathering. You also will want to spend time serving together or supporting each other or your kids at sporting events or school performances and such.

Additionally, commit to loop each other in on a whole host of other normal life rhythms for whoever in your emerging MC wants to jump in or tag along: grocery shopping, taking the kids to the park, a last-minute meal or dessert or movie with one or two others.

Don't treat this like a light switch, something you suddenly flip on in your life. It takes time for any group of people to develop these rhythms and begin to truly feel as if they are part of a family. And it takes an *extra* measure of grace and patience when building an extended family, given the integrations of the various schedules and unique responsibilities everyone has. It also takes great intentionality. These types of rhythms won't just happen, especially at first. You will need to organize some things right off the bat and create space for the more organic rhythms to develop. Remember, slow is fast....

Here are a few sample weekly rhythms to give you a sense of what building a family might look like. These are not a prescription for how to do this, but an idea of how this might *begin* to look:

Sunday	A few folks who are Christians from your MC attend your church's Sunday morning gathering together. Maybe you go out for lunch afterward.
Tuesday	You have a "Family Dinner Night" meal, where everyone in the community is invited and the rings of relationship continue to grow. No pressure, and no agenda other than food and fun.
Wednesday	You send a text out to the guys in your community to see if anyone wants to stop over this evening to watch a game on TV. Three guys jump on the wagon and show up early with snacks galore!
Saturday	Once or twice a month you plan out a way to serve someone or do some sort of restoration project together in your neighborhood.

Here's another example, perhaps for a community that has lots of younger families with kids:

Monday	Three of the young moms in your community get together for a play date with the kids at the park. Often you invite new potential People of Peace to join you.
Tuesday	You send a text to the group letting them know you are going shopping: "Who needs anything while I am out?" Another new friend joins you, as do a couple of single gals who are roommates: "We want to learn how to shop and cook like you do!"
Thursday	You have a "Family Dinner Night" meal that is done "potluck" style, and you come up with a theme for the meal, something like "breakfast for dinner" or "soups and salads." There are lots of kids running around, but a short story and question time is fun and gets everyone to thinking. Everyone helps clean up afterward.
Saturday	Some of the men take the kids out to clean the trails at a local forest preserve while a few others create a simple lunch for everyone who participated to enjoy together.

These are very simple and basic rhythms that pretty much fit into the schedules of your life already. Changing your schedule so you can spend time together is *not* the end game of discipleship, but it is an important beginning as you figure out how life as an extended family can work. Basic "family values" will start to form as you work out details regarding group participation, spontaneous hanging out, sharing of simple meals, and participation in larger and smaller events—both organized and organic.

PROXIMITY IS GOLD

I'm sure you have already figured out that getting into new missional rhythms as an extended family is not without its challenges. It takes great humility and ongoing intentionality to move our own lives and families toward this, and it's exponentially harder when more and more people come into the circle. But don't be discouraged. Remember that all of this is a supernatural work of God, and he *always* fulfills what he commands his people to do. He will lead you through tough spots, fears, and confusion. He is full of grace and never condemns our shortcomings, so we don't need to, either.

One of the challenges you will almost certainly run into as your relational network begins to grow is *proximity*. You will start to bump up against scheduling issues. Distance from one another will seem to prohibit the more organic elements of life together on mission. Proximity is crucial to truly living like a family!

I am often asked if you can start an MC with people who do not live anywhere near each other. Can you have groups that are made up of people who live all over town ... or even farther away? The answer is *yes* ... and *no*.

The real issue behind these questions is, can you live like a close family if you rarely see each other? Well, with enough scheduling and determination you probably can make it work. It is *possible* to live out the more organized aspects of family life, but you are going to have a hard time bringing in the organic aspect of discipleship and mission together. And remember, healthy family life takes both. In my experience, an MC that is made up of people who do not live relatively close to one another will have a very hard time really making disciples and developing others to do the same. Their best intentions usually dissolve into a weekly meeting that they call their "missional community," and it is nothing more than an old-school "small group" with new language and higher hopes. So when it comes to building a family on mission from a *network* or *neighborhood*, I would suggest that you shoot for those closest to you and trust God for growth and multiplication as your collective relational network expands.

The goal is to live like a family on mission together, not just expand your group size.

PROACTIVE AND REACTIVE MISSION

As you go along in life, it will be normal for you to develop relationships with those outside your neighborhood, but collectively, as an MC, you will need to identify your *proactive mission*—those you can and are discipling while doing life together. This is very important. And you will need to learn to trust God with the *reactive mission* opportunities that come up in the flow of life at work or with those outside your closer relational circle. But I want to stress that since the goal of discipleship is to see every part of our lives come in line with the truth of the gospel, being and living more and more like

Jesus, we have to be sure that we are actually in the normal stuff of everyday life with the people we are discipling.[14]

It is one thing to be a witness to someone. It is another thing to disciple them in all of life.

PART OF THE FAMILY

Looking back at how our life as Team K naturally began to pull others in to join our family rhythms, I am reminded how similar life as an MC is to what we experienced together in our family. In many ways, everything we do as an MC today is really just an extension of Team K! The things that God led us to do and share with others have grown and developed in a manner that we never could have predicted, and they have touched people in ways we may never fully know.

In fall 2013 our oldest daughter, Christin, married the love of her life. The entire ceremony and reception was a picture of the gospel. We loved it! During the time when everyone was giving their appropriate—and hilarious—speeches, I stood up and "officially" inducted my new son-in-law, Daniel, into Team K. I had new and improved shirts printed up for him and my daughter. I even threw in a few baby-sized "onesies" with the Team K logo on them. It was all very fun and very intentional. I wanted Daniel to know that we now see him as part of our family in the most intimate of ways—he is now one of us. And I anticipate specific things for them in the future, including adding to the team! We all had a good laugh with many hugs, and we also shared a few tears of joy. Later that night, a very dear friend of ours who was at the wedding posted this on her Facebook page:

Went to a wedding tonight. A very beautiful woman married a very handsome man. There is now a Dillard division of Team K. As one additional member was added to Team K I looked around the room and saw many people I know have been loved and included by every member of that team. There are hundreds of honorary members of Team K and I am blessed beyond words and understanding about how thankful I am to be one of them. Love you all so, so very much and thank you for including, encouraging, and caring for so many.

Thank *you*, Julia, for so beautifully summing up the day for us all. God is good!

Remember, this all starts with *your* family. You will never lead others further or disciple them "better" than you live this out in your own household. This can be challenging for us to get our heads and hearts around, because many of us have built our Christian lives around a Sunday church service or a midweek small group time and an occasional service project. But if you treat discipleship and mission like a weekly meeting or events on a schedule, that's all they will be. And unfortunately, your relationship with God will mirror what you live and practice.

Life with God will be nothing more than a scheduled event, a few times a week.

Small is Big: As you are beginning to live like a *family on mission*, you have probably identified one or two others (individuals or couples) who want to go on mission with you and your family. You will need to be modeling and talking about this life a lot, watching for who is interested in and leaning in to your experience. Begin to introduce them to what you are learning about the gospel and life lived together on mission.

Slow is Fast: Start slowly by having a weekly family dinner together, practicing "What next, Lord?" As a group, ask God to show you how to move toward more intentional discipleship opportunities (like the Story-formed Way) with your People of Peace. Write down what you hear the Spirit saying ... and then do it!

Multiplication Wins: In the next several weeks, look to add another *organized* interaction to your lives together. As you add simple activities to your regular life rhythms, you will begin to see *organic* relational opportunities arise more and more, and close connections with those in your group take root and multiply.

Signpost: Now you're starting to see the rhythms of your life change. Your schedule and resources are beginning to be reoriented toward discipleship and mission with others. New "family values" are beginning to emerge with things like group participation, spontaneous hanging out, simple meals, and participation in both organized and organic activities.

This phase takes *extreme* intentionality for making progress. Your natural patterns and preferences from before will arise to derail you at every turn and need to be confronted (in *your* heart and others') by the gospel. Practice *gospeling* one another often as you grow in gospel fluency.

CHAPTER 6

THE SEED PRINCIPLE

One sure way to get my family and friends out of bed and around the breakfast table is to make a Team K family favorite dish—salami eggs. (Imagine in your mind a plate of food with a glowing orb of joy around it.) This is one of our own concoctions, combining a few different ethnic traditions into one unique and totally delicious meal. Add to this a little breakfast cake, some black coffee, and the occasional mimosa, and an instant brunch-time feast erupts every time.

What's kind of amazing about this particular dish is how many of our friends have started making it themselves, posting pictures online and seeking our vote of approval as they declare this meal to be one of their absolute favorites. Why? Because they've been so blessed by our tradition and want to faithfully pass it on and bless others. It is, in fact, an impossibly easy meal to make—once you've seen it cooked and eaten it a few times. Countless times my wife and I have shown others how many eggs per person to whip up and how to cut the salami into little half-inch squares and fry them *just right* before adding the whipped eggs. We have confided in them which kind of corn and wheat tortillas they should buy to hold the cooked salami and eggs. And we have showed them just the right amount of cream cheese to spread on the tortillas before adding a favorite hot sauce. All of it adds up to one amazing bite of righteousness![1]

To be repeated and passed on, again and again.

This meal has become a ritual, a favored tradition in our household, and now in many others as well. It has multiplied out to new "generations" of salami egg makers, many whom we have never even met. Each one is giving it their unique little spin and nuance, but passing it on faithfully with love.

Imagine if all of life and discipleship followed this same pattern and process.

It can, and it *must*.

Earlier we learned that Jesus' parables and his life with his disciples show us that small is big, slow is fast, and that applying these truths always leads to multiplication and abundance in the kingdom. Now I want to take a little more time to look at the idea of multiplication being seeded into everything we do. It's critical that we not only learn to live as extended families on mission, but faithfully and intentionally pass this way of living on to other disciples, who in turn make more disciples.

A LIVING EXAMPLE

Beyond just teaching principles to his disciples, Jesus spent time living with them and showing them what life in the king-

dom of God looks like. He gave them opportunities to participate in these kingdom realities. We see all of this played out
beautifully in a nuts-and-bolts account given by the gospel
writer Mark.[2] He tells of the time when Jesus and the boys
had been teaching large crowds of people for three days and
everyone was starting to get really hungry. This had happened
at least once before, and at that time Jesus multiplied a few
loaves of bread and a couple of small fish into a banquet large
enough to feed more than five thousand people. This time
Jesus tells his disciples that if these folks don't get something
to eat soon, they will all pass out on the way home.

His knucklehead disciples respond, "What do you expect *us*
to do about it way out here in the desert?" They bring Jesus
what they have — seven loaves of bread — and he prays over
them and breaks the bread into pieces, asking the disciples
to start passing it out to the crowd of around four thousand
people. The disciples manage to scrounge up a few small fish
as well, so Jesus blesses what they found and has them start to
distribute them also. Amazingly, everyone eats their fill — and
beyond. Jesus sends the crowds on their way with full bellies,
and the leftovers fill up seven large baskets. Pretty cool!

Later, after Jesus and his crew have rowed over to the other
side of the lake, the disciples are arguing among themselves
because they had forgotten to bring any of the extra food
along, and it is getting to be that time again. They find a
single loaf of bread in the boat, but that is it.

> Jesus knew what they were saying, so he said, "Why are you
> arguing about having no bread? Don't you know or under-
> stand even yet? Are your hearts too hard to take it in? 'You have
> eyes — can't you see? You have ears — can't you hear?' Don't
> you remember anything at all? When I fed the 5,000 with five

loaves of bread, how many baskets of leftovers did you pick up afterward?"

"Twelve," they said.

"And when I fed the 4,000 with seven loaves, how many large baskets of leftovers did you pick up?"

"Seven," they said.

"Don't you understand yet?" he asked them.[3]

This story really encourages me. Even though Jesus is the perfect teacher, we see here that it takes considerable time for his disciples to really grasp what they have just seen and experienced. A *small* amount of food had been *multiplied* (twice) into a feast. But the disciples were very *slowly* coming to a full understanding of how the kingdom works. Notice, too, the normalcy of the setting for them. They are teaching in both crowds and in a small circle of friends. A meal is always involved. Questions are asked from both sides. Growth is happening over time with learning connected to practice. This is key.

If discipleship worked that way for Jesus, we should buckle up and be prepared for it to work that way in our life and community too.

AS YOU GO

Being a disciple is part of our transformed, called-out identity. It is *who we are*, and out of this *being* we live as disciples who make disciples. Each of us has many different roles in life. Mine include being a father, husband, home owner, pastor, author, and so on. I don't stop being a father while I am writing a book. I don't push the pause button on my role as a husband while working on projects around the house. In the same way, I never stop being a disciple or discipling others—segmenting discipleship into a certain part of my life but not others. What this means is that I will be going about all the normal stuff of my life, meeting my responsibilities as a father, businessman, husband, etc., *as a disciple* who is making disciples.

I have spent time weeding my gardens, painting my house, fixing plumbing leaks, and doing a million other things as I've "discipled" others in community. We have spent countless hours together discussing every conceivable topic, much of it in light of the gospel and what the Bible has to say about life, while working at everyday, normal things. We cannot accurately discern a person's heart and character while just sitting in a series of classes or by only reading through materials together—but we can when we're all tired and there's more work to be done.

How many of us would see a project on a to-do list as a *perfect* opportunity for discipleship? A couple of summers ago my deck was in major need of repair and re-staining. It was a huge job because I have a huge deck! But as they say, many hands make light work, and there were several people I really wanted to be spending time with, so I called a few of them up and asked if they wanted to "hang out."

"Awesome, stop by tomorrow morning around nine … and by the way, wear some old clothes that you don't mind getting dirty.…"

The first to arrive was Jake, a young leader who was pretty new to our community and a really cool guy. I wanted to get to know him better, and I wanted to see if he had a servant's heart. I explained in great detail *exactly* how I wanted him to paint the spindles of the handrail around my deck. I pointed out that the decking had just been refinished and therefore he must be extremely careful not to drip paint on it while applying the three different colors of paint that went onto the handrails. His eyes widened as he wondered what he had gotten himself into.

I told him that I was *extremely* picky and wanted this done very well—but that I loved him more than my deck and was grateful for his help. "Do your best, and we'll be good to go, brother!"

As I got back to work, I watched Jake work too.

He did an amazing job, being extra careful. He stopped a few times to get my feedback and see if he was doing it the way I wanted. I gave him a few pointers on how to get the corners right and a trick or two to make it quicker, assuring him he was doing a great job. As others in our community showed up to help, it was Jake who took them aside and explained *exactly* how he was doing this, gave them a few pointers, and then looped back to check on their work as they painted. The job was finished in about a third of the time it would have taken me to do it alone. And as we had a few beers and some pizza together, I gave the group feedback on what I had observed in them today, thanking them and encouraging them.

In getting my project finished I was also able to watch Jake and others serve in humility and grace, sticking around until the job was finished and having a great time doing it. I also watched as Jake passed on to others what he had learned. One of the single women who was there had just bought her first home and told us she was glad to have learned what she did that day because she had a lot of painting that needed to be done at her place too.

We all offered to help her get it done in the weeks ahead.

RE-PARENTING A CULTURE

As I grow in this life of living like an extended family on mission, I am increasingly struck by how many of the things that my wife and I did with our own kids as they grew up are the same things that we find ourselves replicating with others now in our missional community. For instance, early in their lives we taught our children how to set up a personal budget and decide how they would spend their money, asking for God's guidance and wisdom. We taught them to be patient and the difference between "wants" and "needs."

We have now done the same thing with many from our missional community.

We trained our children how to serve others in our extended family through babysitting, cooking meals, cleaning houses, or raking leaves. Many in our community have learned to work hard and serve others out of a grateful heart for the service they have received from Christ. I taught my son and daughters how to fix their bikes, stop a leak, paint a wall, and properly clean up when the job is finished. Over the years in community we have had to teach myriads of young people all of these same things as they started families and new MCs.

Tina spent years teaching all three of our kids (and me) how to cook. Not just how to follow recipes, but how to shop, get deals, repurpose leftovers, and really spread the love and hospitality in ways that bless others and make them feel welcome. Our kids are now grown and throw *the best* parties and are all incredible cooks in their own right! And so are many in our extended family who have learned from Tina and now have the skills and confidence to serve others this way, pass on what they've learned (like salami eggs), and continue traditions that we modeled and established in their lives.

I consistently dated my girls while they were growing up. From the time they were two or three years old, they would dress up and pick their favorite place to eat dinner (usually crummy fast food when they were young), and I would take them out, separately, on dates. I would open doors for them, displaying my best chivalry and manners. They would ask me lots of questions, and we would laugh and have so much fun together. I would tell them how beautiful they were and how awesome it was to have this time for just the two of us. "You are special, honey, and I love you and God loves you!"

I will never forget how our daughter Christin, at the age of four, helped her younger sister, Justine, who was two at the time, prepare for her first date night with me. Christin helped her pick out a dress and shoes, loaned her a favorite plastic pearl necklace, and told her which restaurant she should have me take her to. Justine beamed with a smile as wide as the sky when she emerged from her room ready for our first date. Awesome! I have tears in my eyes as I recall that day.

My wife did the same thing with our son throughout the years, teaching him how to be a gentleman, how to eat with proper manners, and how to treat a girl appropriately as she dated him.

We have had to teach and model these same exact things with many young men and women in our community. So many have never been taught these factors or learned how to view all of life through the lens of the gospel. Discipleship includes seeding kingdom multiplication into every area of life, not just teaching the Bible and theology. In many ways, discipleship is a re-parenting of others, showing them how to live in God's family in light of what our Father now says is true of them.

HEALTHY THINGS GROW

Everything God created has the seed of multiplication built into it: plants, animals, humans, families, communities, and the church. This in many ways is the story line of the Bible. God blessed Adam and Eve and sent them to be fruitful and multiply and fill the earth.[4] And when God restarted all of humanity through Noah and his family, he commanded them to be fruitful and multiply and increase the number of people exponentially.[5] When God changed Jacob's name to Israel and confirmed his calling, reaffirming his covenant to Abraham and his people, God said to him, "I am God Almighty: be fruitful and multiply."[6] As Jesus sent his disciples out into the world on his great, eternal mission, he commissioned them with the same command: Go and make disciples all over the world![7]

When it comes to discipleship and the growth of missional communities, multiplication doesn't just happen accidentally. Everything we do must be intentionally simple, scalable, and reproducible. If we are not careful, our communities will remain or revert back to inward-focused "small groups," Bible studies, or self-help circles.

WHY MULTIPLY?

The prophet Habakkuk declared the Father's vision for the earth when he said, "For the earth will be filled with the knowledge of the glory of the LORD as the waters cover the sea."[8] As we multiply and expand the church—as disciples of Jesus are becoming more like him and making more disciples—God's glory is multiplied. The writer of Hebrews said that Jesus is the radiance of his Father's glory and the exact imprint of his nature.[9] It is the purpose and plan of the gospel that more and more of Jesus' life and ministry, through his disciples, fill every nook and cranny, family and neighborhood—every nation on the planet!

> And we, who with unveiled faces all reflect the Lord's glory, are being transformed into his image with ever-increasing glory, which comes from the Lord, who is the Spirit.[10]

> Praise be to his glorious name forever; may the whole earth be filled with his glory. Amen and Amen.[11]

IT'S JUST TOO BIG

Most people cannot multiply or replicate what they experience on Sundays at a church service. If what we teach, preach, and train others in cannot be reproduced immediately, over and over, then it will never lead to growth and multiplication. So what are those "biggies" that we must be sure are seeded into our lives and the lives of others for multiplication? There are different ways of saying this or grouping these teachings and practices together, but there are three main components that must be taught, lived out, modeled, reminded, and retaught over and over: *gospel, community,* and *mission.*

These three elements are the foundation, the core we return to, that consistently helps disciples connect to God in every area of their lives. We need to help people increase in the rhythms of living out the *gospel* together in *community,* living more and more like a family. And it takes consistent growth in the *mission* of pursuing people who are not yet part of the family and seeking those God has specifically called us to make disciples of.

My friends Hugh Halter and Matt Smay help lead Adullam, a church made up of missional communities in Denver, and they help people envision it this way:

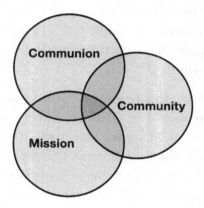

Hugh and Matt teach that discipleship and multiplication occur when we see the intersection of communion with God and growth in the gospel, life lived in community where the gospel is increasingly lived out, and an intentional focus on reaching outward toward those not yet in the community.[12]

Mike and Sally Breen, two close friends who are also master disciple makers, paint the picture using a simple shape to help their disciples remember this dynamic:

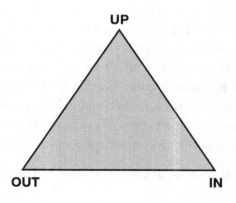

They explain that Jesus was careful to balance his life between his relationship with his Father (UP), his relationship with his spiritual family (IN), and his relationship and time spent with broken people who did not yet know the love of his Father or the encouragement of his family (OUT). As disciples of Jesus, we must regularly calibrate these up/in/out expressions in our own communities.[13]

Whichever way is most helpful for you to understand these elements is great, but regardless of the visual model you embrace, the truth remains: you need all three elements. We cannot lead others to become mature disciples of Jesus without these three components working in conjunction with one another. Discipleship happens in a gospel-centered community that is living life together on mission. This is because a community that does not have the gospel as its center and purpose is just another social group or club. And it's when we really live out Jesus' mission that our true need for him and the gospel is revealed in greater ways. The Spirit uses these experiences and the various parts of the body in our community to help us conform to Christ. This is how true discipleship happens — not in a classroom, but in a family of missionary servants.

Everything we have learned to this point has shown us that discipleship is not simply an individual reality, but also a communal one. In fact, Jesus never intended his disciples to go and live out a *personal* faith on a *personal* mission all alone. Our identity in Christ is an identity best understood and expressed in community. It is when we live and work together in a bond of love and unity that all the parts of Jesus' body (the church) come together into a glorious display of what he is like.

To get a grasp on this, ask yourself these questions:

Gospel: Are people being trained in their "gospel fluency"? How can we help people grow in the gospel in ways that they understand and can reproduce naturally?

Community: Is the way we live as an *oikos*—an extended family—easily and naturally reproducible by everyone and in any context?

Mission: Have we kept the mission of making disciples clear and up-front, and is it seen as something organic, as a part of everyday life?

If you get this right and seed the multiplication of these foundational elements into everything you do, you will make great strides toward growth and reproduction. Of course, there are many different topics and teachings that go into the full picture of making mature disciples. The process ultimately takes a lifetime. And given the scope of this chapter and the space it would require, we won't exhaustively look at everything that goes into discipleship, but for now take a look at this list and begin to think about how you would teach and model these things in ways that are reproducible by others:

- Gospel fluency

- Soul care

- Conflict resolution

- Hospitality

- Finances and generosity

- Time management / work ethic

- Parenting skills

- Biblical marriage

- Bible knowledge (how to read and understand the Word)

  Note: Check out the Resource Toolbox in Appendix C to find resources connected to all of these topics.

All of this falls under the broader categories of gospel, community, and mission, but notice how many of these things can only be taught and reproduced in normal life as others observe and participate in your life.

GET A RHYTHM

I have learned that the secret to increasingly living our lives together on God's mission is to move away from seeing discipleship as something that needs to be tacked onto an already busy schedule, toward seeing all the normal stuff of life as full of opportunity for discipleship and growth in the gospel.

This is not a call to life *plus* mission; rather, it is a call to life *on* mission.

We have discovered six common rhythms that are found in every context and culture that we can intentionally engage in for the sake of making disciples. I have found that these six rhythms have been like handles I can hold onto, rather than a missional to-do list. In many ways you may already be living in some of these rhythms and just not have noticed. As you read through them, think about what each one might look like for you as a part of your daily and weekly cadence of life.[14]

Know the Story

Everyone has a story (or many stories) to tell; we are "story-formed" people. Make it a habit to get to know the stories of the people in your life and community. They are dying to tell you! Help others to see how their stories intersect with and mirror God's story. In order to grow in this ability—to listen and connect the stories of people with the story of God—you will need to get more familiar with the narrative of the Bible and God's story.[15] There are some great resources to help you do this that we will talk about later.

Listen

We are all listening to something or someone. Set aside regular times to just *listen* to God. Try having times of prayer where all you do is listen for the voice of God to speak, resisting the urge to give God your to-do list. Regularly practice listening "backward" by spending time in God's Word. And actively listen "forward" to hear what God is saying to you today through his Spirit and through your community. God is waiting to talk with us.

Eat

Regularly eat meals with others as a reminder of our common need for God and his faithfulness to provide for us both physically and spiritually. You are probably already eating around twenty-one meals each week. Start by consistently having at least one meal each week with a not-yet believer. Frequently invite others to have a seat at your Father's table!

Bless

God desires that all nations—all people—would be blessed through Jesus. Seek God's direction for whom he would have you tangibly bless each week. Intentionally bless others through words, gifts, and actions. You will be amazed at how many opportunities there are and what a difference it makes when a community is consistently blessing those around them.

Celebrate

Everyone is celebrating something—join them! Make celebrations and parties that you already attend a way to share the generosity God has shown you. Gather consistently throughout the week with your community to share stories and celebrate all that God is doing in and among you. Invite others to these celebrations as a way of displaying God's extravagant blessings.

ReCreate

Take time each week to rest, play, create, and restore beauty in ways that display the gospel, resting in Jesus' completed work on your behalf. Cultivate this gospel rhythm of rest and create—*ReCreate*—in your life. This is truly what it means to "keep the Sabbath."

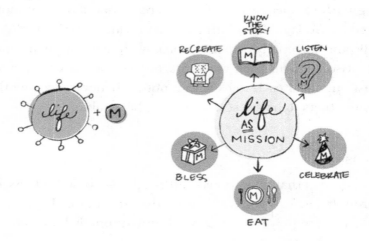

Each of these rhythms can be practiced in your life individually as well as in community, and they will help establish new *organized* opportunities for mission as well as occasions to be more present and find opportunities to share and model the gospel in more *organic* ways. You might find it helpful to post these "rhythms" somewhere to remind you of these easy, daily opportunities you have to live out your gospel identity. What I am suggesting here is "recycling" your time: looking at the activities and normal stuff of life you are already involved in and seeking to bring a greater gospel and missional focus to them rather than adding more events and extra commitments to the calendar.[16]

If life on mission, a life of discipleship, is too hard, or seems impossible with your schedule . . .

Choose a different rhythm.[17]

RAISE THE KIDS TO MOVE OUT

As you lead others in community, it will be important not only to plan multiplication into everything you do, but also to clearly plant the *expectation* of multiplication. Remember, healthy things grow, expand, and take new ground. You would never want your kids to grow up and *not* have a family and kids of their own, staying in your house and being cared for as children forever.

That would be weird and a little twisted.

When my son was a boy, I taught him to mow the lawn and use basic tools, telling him that someday he would be a man with a family of his own and he would need these skills. I seeded in his heart and mind an expectation that he would likely be a father and lead his own family at some point in the future.

It's the same with growth and leadership in our missional communities.

We need to expect growth and multiplication to happen while letting everyone involved know that this is normal and good. And just like when our children become adults, leave home, and start families of their own, there is a grieving process that rightfully occurs when we send "family members" off on mission. Embrace this grief. Grief is not a bad thing. We mourn change, but change in this case shows growth, progress, and God's blessings. Talk about this early on, helping your community to see multiplication as not only natural, but also essential to accomplishing the mission.

In the next chapter we will take this one step further and look at one of the most important aspects of reproduction: the multiplication of leaders. This area is often overlooked or assumed until the need for new leaders smacks us in the face and we realize we have not planned well. At some point you will realize that you need new leaders who will start new missional communities. Will you be ready when that happens?

THE SEED PRINCIPLE   **129**

Small is Big: There is no more important *small is big* principle than growing in *gospel*, *community*, and *mission*. Connecting deeper with God, his community, and those he is sending you to is central to discipleship. What is one "up," "in," and "out" activity you can begin to grow in at this point?

Slow is Fast: Which of the discipleship rhythms in your life are shifting from being "additional" to "intentional"? Each week try to add slowly, but with intentionality, one more of the "rhythms" shared above. Discuss with your community how each of these can be a living demonstration of the gospel in everyday life.

Multiplication Wins: Have you begun to develop a Community Covenant yet? Actually spending the time to write out the ways you intend to live out your new community identity on mission together is critical to getting to multiplication. Check out the resource in Appendix C and begin to go through this together as a community — or start with just your family — but now is the time to bring greater intentionality and accountability into the picture.

Signpost: At this point along the road you probably have a few or quite a few other people or families starting to live on mission with you. If it is starting to feel like a busy, heavy burden, then it may be that you are not seeing the gospel transforming others in community or that you are trying to do everything for everyone. You are not everyone's savior, parent, or housekeeper! Look for simple reproducibility in everything you do at this point. Remember to not only "do" lots of missional things with or in front of people, but teach them the gospel motivation behind it and how they can use tools and ideas such as "Up, In, Out" or "What Next, Lord?" in their own lives.

CHAPTER 7

YEAST IN THE DOUGH

We own a breakfast café in Tacoma, and it's a hoppin' place. We usually have a line out the door on weekends with people gladly waiting to get in to enjoy a favorite dish, swap stories, and reconnect with the community at large. There is always something more for our super-busy staff to do. Often they are so hard at work that they can think of little more than getting their job done and making it through another shift. But some of the staff "lean in" to opportunities for additional training and the chance to move up to better positions.

Joey is one of these people. He started working for us as a dishwasher when he was seventeen years old, and he quickly learned the ropes, moving up to clearing and busing tables for the waitstaff. He asked if we would train him to be a waiter as well. Joey wants to learn how to be a barista and make all of our specialty coffees. He has told us that he wants to learn *every job* there is at Shakabrah, our café, because he hopes to own the place someday. He always gives his best and has a great attitude about working hard. He loves his job and the family he has found among us, and we love him too.

I hope that someday Joey does own Shakabrah!

We offer to cross-train all of our employees in areas that they don't work in. Some lean in and learn, but most don't. I don't say this to set up a contrast between the "heroes" and "losers"; rather, I simply want to illustrate that there are some who show the desire and capacity to learn and apply new things *right now.* When looking to develop leaders, we initially have to identify who *wants* to lead. We do this by looking at who is ready first to be a *follower.*

CROP VERSUS YEAST

Far too many people, when first embarking on life in a discipling community, become singularly focused on the acquisition and reproduction of knowledge and worry too much about "group dynamics." But if all of our efforts never lead to new leaders being sent out on mission to start new extended families (*oikos*), then we just become another self-focused group that never grows. Or perhaps we become intoxicated with our group just getting larger and larger under our own leadership and direct supervision. Remember, healthy things always grow *and* reproduce themselves. If your missional community grows larger but never multiplies, it is not healthy.

In my earliest experiences with starting MCs and planting churches, I learned that I had to keep my eye on the prize of ongoing leadership development. It had to remain a high priority. We equipped *everyone* in community in the same way as we tried to raise a new crop of leaders. And we learned the hard way that not everyone was willing or able to lead, and certainly not in the same ways. Instead of trying to raise a *crop*, we needed to shift our focus to finding the *yeast* that could be worked into and affect the entire lump of doughy community. What do I mean by that?

This should not have come as such a revelation to us because Jesus taught just such a thing to his disciples. In back-to-back parables he contrasted the difference between the growing of crops and the effect of yeast in baking bread and how these apply to kingdom principles for growth.

> "The Kingdom of Heaven is like a farmer who planted good seed in his field. But that night as the workers slept, his enemy came and planted weeds among the wheat, then slipped away. When the crop began to grow and produce grain, the weeds also grew.
>
> "The farmer's workers went to him and said, 'Sir, the field where you planted that good seed is full of weeds! Where did they come from?'
>
> "'An enemy has done this!' the farmer exclaimed.
>
> "'Should we pull out the weeds?' they asked.
>
> "'No,' he replied, 'you'll uproot the wheat if you do. Let both grow together until the harvest. Then I will tell the harvesters to sort out the weeds, tie them into bundles, and burn them, and to put the wheat in the barn.'"[1]

So the farmer in this illustration — whom I'll call a disciple maker — plants good seed, but not everything that comes up in the field is equal to or necessarily the desired result. The same working of the field did not produce the same exact results of intended growth.

Now, in between this parable and the next one is a short parable we have already looked at. It's where Jesus tells us that the kingdom of God is like a mustard seed. It is really small at first, but then grows into a large tree where many come to find shelter. Notice that Jesus is shifting from a crop illustration to one that shows the smaller and rarer component having greater results. Then he goes on with another parable:

> "The Kingdom of Heaven is like the yeast a woman used in making bread. Even though she put only a little yeast in three measures of flour, it permeated every part of the dough."[2]

Here Jesus tells us that just a little yeast can change everything and lead to great expansion of the community—or should I say "dough." He shifts from the perspective of raising crops, where the result is mixed, to using yeast, which permeates an entire loaf of bread. As we apply this to leadership development, I believe it means that it's possible to apply a common, one-size-fits-all approach in trying to raise a crop of "leaders," but you rarely get the same fruitfulness out of each person. By contrast, looking for the "yeasty" people, those who are ready for growth and will in turn lead others to maturity along with them, produces a far greater result. And I can tell you, it is a pleasure giving time and energy to those who desire to be equipped to lead. It's much easier than trying to develop folks who are not interested, ready, or positioned for growth.

One is a blessing, and the other always feels like heavy lifting.

Another thing to point out here: Jesus instructed his disciples that they were not to tear out the shoots that were not wheat, but to leave them in the field (community). He didn't want them to accidentally rip out or damage any of the crops, knowing that it can be hard at times to tell a young wheat shoot from a weed. So as you seek to develop those who will be lead-disciplers in your community, it's important to continue to love *everyone* while calling them to greater maturity and kingdom activity.

Jesus preached to the crowds, taught those who followed him, and discipled those who were humble and obedient.

In the gospel of Mark we hear the account of a rich, influential young man who approaches Jesus with a desire to be a part of the kingdom. The narrative says that after hearing the man's insistence that he had kept the Law and was ready for a position in the kingdom, "Jesus looked at him and loved him."[3] Jesus then challenged the man to lay down the things he currently valued most in his life, and we see the man walk off sad, knowing that he was not ready for that level of commitment.

Not everyone will follow and submit to discipleship. Not everyone will lead. Yet we are called to love all whom God brings into our circle of influence and extended family. It will quickly become apparent who is ready to go to the next level with us.

STRAIGHT FROM THE HORSE'S MOUTH

I would like to give you another perspective on all of this from the seat of one who was discipled and developed as a leader within one of our missional communities. Randy Sheets is a great guy and a good friend of mine. He first became a part of our church community, Soma,[4] after finding us through a friend and coming to one of our Sunday morning gatherings where several of our missional communities come together for worship, teaching, food, and celebration. Randy has consistently been a follower and leaned into those around him from whom he could learn. He is a servant and has become a strong leader within our larger community. Here's a conversation I recently had with this spiritual brother:

> **Caesar:** After getting to know a few people within the community, what shifted for you that took you from "casual observer" to being part of the community yourself? What was it you were looking for at the time?
>
> **Randy:** It wasn't anything big or far-reaching like church-planting goals or some big ministry dream. I felt as if God had told me I would lead some day in the church and at that time I was enrolled in seminary. I was looking for a mentored life. There has to be more than just going to church, right?
>
> I met Jeff Vanderstelt [another Soma pastor], and he pursued me and asked me to join his DNA group with a couple other guys. It was in those times of growing relationship, trust, and accountability that Jeff challenged us a lot with the implications of the gospel, our views on things, and the choices we were making in life. I started to build relationships with others in his MC and started hanging out and being a part of everything that they were doing and experiencing. I saw that there was something these people knew and lived out that I wanted to have and live out too. I also needed examples and a greater understanding of how to live and be a man, a husband, and a father.
>
> **Caesar:** Tell me what you remember and how it felt when you first started living in community and being discipled as a lifestyle.
>
> **Randy:** It first looked like backwards growth to me. I felt like the worst Christian ever as I realized the sin in my heart that was being exposed over and over. It was brutal! I couldn't run away from it, because I was around people so much in every aspect of my life, and

they were living differently and exposing my own actions, my heart, and the way I was treating my girlfriend Lisa. [Lisa is now Randy's wife, and they are raising a growing family.] More than anything, I realized that my heart was gross in a lot of areas.

I would get jealous when someone else spoke with wisdom or seemed to have greater maturity or victory in an area of their life than I did. When someone would let me down, which happens all the time in community, I would feel real anger toward them. I started to learn that my sense of joy and peace was connected to the approval or opinions of others, and I would feel terrible if someone was disappointed in me. Which can also happen a lot in community.

Going through the Story-formed Way in my MC caused me to wrestle with these things in my heart. The gospel was being applied to every area of my life, and in our group discussion and interactions, people were starting to call me out; practically, verbally, but also with the example of their lives. Those were some tough times, but looking back, they were God's grace and blessing for me for sure.

Caesar: What did your "leadership training" look like at that point? How was it being delivered to you?

Randy: The ideas of what seminary was supposed to do, and how it would shape my life, started to crumble for me. The simplicity and profoundness of the Story experienced in community was changing me more than all my classes at school. Sitting in a living room, having meals with messy people, serving together, times with my DNA group, other one-to-one times ... Learning how to cook a meal, what to serve, and how it could all be a huge picture of the gospel in action ... was life changing. Doing dishes after meals could change your opinion or wrongly held view forever! Lisa was living with the Vanderstelts at this time, and I/we experienced real-time, up-close, and personal training in what a biblical marriage and home could look like, and how to fight and seek forgiveness. How to love and discipline kids in light of the gospel. And there was always a celebration with lots of people around.

I remember these times with Randy in our community. He began to soak in any informal or formal training that Jeff, I, and other Soma leaders offered. He read every book we mentioned. He showed up to everything he was invited to participate in. He would help with yard work, house repairs, and moving people's things from place to place. Randy rarely missed a time to go to the gym or drive leaders to and from the airport, just to have time to ask questions and learn.

Caesar: What opportunities were you given to begin to pass on what you had experienced and been taught?

Randy: It was always seeded into us/me that we were experiencing this time and discipleship to get on mission and do the same with others. This isn't just for yourself, for your growth. Initially I thought, "I need to get more knowledge ..." But the longer I hung around, the more I realized that the gospel was changing me, and all of this was for my community and others — this was not just about me and my life!

I started helping out with middle-school-aged kids that were a part of our larger Soma family, and Lisa and I took them through the Story-formed Way at a local café. After about a year and a half of life in our missional community, a few of us were "sent" by the group to start our own MC, focused specifically on making disciples of college students in Tacoma. At first it seemed pretty smooth, but before long I realized I was not very good at all of this yet. I still had a lot to learn. But the best way for me to continue to learn and grow at this point was to begin to lead others. Crazy how that works!

Caesar: Looking back now, what would you like to have received and experienced more of during your ongoing discipleship and leadership development?

Randy: If there were some way to have had a more well-defined pathway for each level of discipleship and leadership and the steps to becoming an MC leader, that would have been helpful. I know something like that could become a "to-do list" and my heart could try and make progress for all the wrong reasons, but the way I'm wired, I think it would have been helpful.

I received a lot of coaching along the way, and still do, but a very clear and consistent coaching system that connected teachings/ trainings to the next steps of my leadership and addressed areas of my strengths and weaknesses would have helped me lead others much better, especially in the beginning. Even though I may act like "I've got this" at times, as a new MC leader I really needed continual feedback, review ... correction. Early on I wasn't as clear as I could have been on how one thing leads to the next ... to multiplication ... to church planting. I want to do my best to make sure those I'm now leading know how the whole big picture fits together.

After this interview I apologized to Randy that I had not done as well as I could have in some of these areas, and I let him know that his feedback was super helpful for me, even today. Learn forward ... right? As we wrap this up, I want to boast a little about how God is using Randy and Lisa in the lives of many people today. Their MC has grown incredibly in their gospel fluency, and they have seen people coming to faith and being baptized into their new identity in Christ. And Randy now helps give leadership and oversight to our larger Soma family in Tacoma and has worked with others to create a summer-long internship for college students from all over the world.

Keep going, brother ... I love you!

4 GEN EXPLOSION

As you can see, your time spent developing and equipping the right people can have immediate and expansive results. Leadership development is really just discipleship further along the path of faith, knowledge, and skills. If you have trained people in such a way that they can now reproduce and disciple others, in turn producing future leaders, you have the makings of a true kingdom movement.

When I teach my kids what I learned from my mother or father, and they in turn teach these same things to their own kids, that encompasses four generations of my family: my parents, my wife and I, my children, and their kids. This is a picture of how multiplication operates. It moves naturally and quickly from one generation to the next and has the ability to impact the future in powerful ways.

The apostle Paul once said to his apprentice Timothy, "The things you have heard me say in the presence of many witnesses entrust to reliable people who will also be qualified to teach others."[5] Paul, Timothy, reliable people, others. Again, we see four generations and a natural pattern. For years when I read this passage, this simple yet powerful blueprint escaped me. It seemed natural when I read it, but I didn't immediately grasp the explosive implication found here. One generation of people is generally considered to cover around twenty-five years of time or history. Four generations therefore encompasses about a hundred years.

Whoa!

Many sociologists point out that throughout history we tend to see major shifts in culture and worldview approximately every four generations. If we want to change a city or a nation, and we can immediately touch the next three generations of disciples (four including ourselves), we will see amazing multiplication that can have an incredible impact on the world. Just by being intentional in passing on reproducible discipleship in *all* of life, we each have the potential to shift and influence the next one hundred years and beyond. But this doesn't have to take a whole century to become a visible reality. When you get to the fourth generation of reproduction in your missional communities and the process of disciples making disciples, things are now fueled by new traditions, and a culture itself takes flight.

That's some powerful stuff.

LEADERS OF PEACE

In a sense, the same People of Peace principles apply when you are looking for leaders to whom to give more of your time and focus. Who are those men and women in your extended family that are "leaning in" to everything you do as a leader? Who are those that are always looking to lend you a hand or serve others? Which people take what you teach and really run with it and apply it to their lives and immediately share these things with those around them?

These are the ones you really want to pour into. These are the ones who will be a *pleasure* to lead and give your life to because they are hungry and faithful.

5 Cs

So who specifically are you looking to develop as your next generation of leaders? Do you have someone in mind yet?

How will you know when you see them and that they are truly good yeast? Let me suggest five qualities to look for in people who are potential leaders. They all start with the letter *C*. The first four are Character, Chemistry, Capacity, and Calling.

Character: Does this person have the personal spiritual and emotional life needed by someone who is going to live on mission and lead others? Do they at least have the desire to develop it? Do they hear from God in prayer and respond in obedience? Do they have good follow-through, letting their yes be a "yes and done"? Do they do the right thing regardless of reward or recognition?

Chemistry: Do you and others like hanging out with this person? Do people enjoy working with him or her? Would you trust this person to have your back when challenging situations arise or spiritual attack is evident?

Capacity: Does this person have the necessary time in their current schedule or season of life to lead others? Are they physically and emotionally healthy? Do they react well under stress and when people and things get difficult?

Calling: Is this person called to this *specific* work at this *specific* time? Are these the people and place they are called to make disciples among? Do they know their role in the community?[6]

You may have noticed that I've placed a great deal of emphasis on a person's character. Because character can and must be continually developed in a leader, if they do not *presently* demonstrate a fairly mature character, it is a signal to wait on pouring your best leadership development time into them. Poor character leads to all sorts of yet-to-be-discovered problems.

A leader with bad character is not the type of yeast you want in your dough.[7]

I promised five Cs, so as a bonus to round it out, here is the fifth: *Competency.* This is something that can be developed in any person who has character and capacity. In my experience, those with high capacity are continuous learners and develop new competencies all the time. I put competency at the end of the list because, to be honest, it is something of a "second tier" concern. It matters, but not as much as the others. Still, if you want to begin measuring this aspect of leadership, you can look at the following: Does this person have some recognized gifting and skills that they use to serve others? Are their goals for leadership in line with these gifts? Does this person regularly pursue growth in their existing strengths *and* areas of weakness?

GETTING MAWL'D

Regardless of what knowledge, skill, or spiritual practice you want to impart to your leaders or see them begin to master and then pass on to others, you will need a process that helps ensure the transfer and reproduction you are hoping for. Years ago John Witte, a foreign missionary friend of mine, dropped this well-proven method on me: MAWL. It's an acronym that stands for *model, assist, watch,* and *leave.* Let me break it down for you a little.

Model: People need to hear you, see you, experience you living out and modeling the things that you want them to learn, to get to the point of reproducing those things in others. They will also need a method to pass it on to the next generation, so MAWL actually models this for them too.

> *Challenge:* You will need to be sure to make everything simple and reproducible, explaining why you are doing what

you do. Don't miss this! Leaders will also need to have access to you in order to actually see you model this lifestyle. This process is not reserved for "formal teaching" moments; leaders should see you model all of the life skills needed to be and make mature disciples.

Assist: After your leaders have seen you do something for a while, it is time for you to assist them as they begin to lead in this area. Additionally, they might continue on this trail of learning by assisting you for a while as you lead.

> *Challenge:* Skills take time to develop; be patient and super encouraging. If you don't help them do things in the ways you hope to reproduce, they will be left to wing it for themselves and may lose the ethos or essence of what it is you are hoping to transfer to them. You are making another original disciple — not a second- (or third-) generation photocopy!

Watch: Now you step back and watch your apprentice do or lead the very things they have seen you do and have been assisted in learning and living out. Often at this point you are letting this person lead *you* in this area or activity.

> *Challenge:* It can be hard not to interfere and instead let others do things that you know you could do better. Trust God here. We all learn best by "doing," followed by encouragement and correction. Be sure to give feedback to your leaders, starting with the positive, and then discuss areas you think they could improve in. Loop back and revisit them periodically to give further encouragement or course correction to ensure that they are faithfully reproducing the things you have taught them.

Leave: Eventually you will need to leave these leaders alone to lead in your community or send them off to multiply the very skills and aspects of this missionary life with which you have equipped them. If you have walked through the first three steps (model, assist, watch), then this step is crucial to their maturity and the expansion of God's kingdom.

> *Challenge:* If you don't leave or send them to lead new missional communities, they will stay dependent on you just as when they were "young" disciples. You will never get to kingdom movement and expansion, and the mission will stay at the size and pace that you can manage alone. Not good!

The church has commonly required people to have a very high level of education and proven experience before they release them to lead and multiply. MAWL your people and release them to lead! Leadership development, as I said earlier, is actually just discipleship further up the slope, walking with people longer and deeper into the ways of Jesus and the kingdom of God. Making mature disciples who lead others will include more experience and time, and greater trust must be built in both directions, but it is basically discipleship over the long haul. Use the MAWL process in everything you do with all the disciples in your life.

Releasing new leaders and watching them begin to lead is their fastest road to growth—and that's true for you as well. As we submit ourselves to learning from others who are wiser than we are, we model Jesus' heart and submission to his Father. *"I only do what I have seen the Father do...."*[8] Being God, Jesus nevertheless learned and grew and taught others. We must have the same humbleness of heart to continue to grow and lead others to maturity.

A MODERN PARABLE

There was an MC leader who went dejectedly crying to his coach. He complained that after all the work he had poured into another couple, his apprentices, they had decided to leave the community and move to another city. It happened pretty suddenly, without much discussion, and now they had just announced that they were moving next month. The leader voiced concern, wondering if the couple had ever really bought into living life together on mission. "What should I do? I feel like giving up ... I'm not very good at this discipleship and mission stuff. It would just be easier if a handful of us stuck it out and lived life together."

The wise and experienced coach told the man that he could help him solve his problem. "Go find another community leader who has never had another person or couple leave their community or had their leadership called into question. When you find this leader, borrow their Bible from them and bring it to me."

The hopeful leader searched diligently, speaking to everyone else he knew who was living with others on mission, but to his disappointment, he could find no other leader with those credentials. Finally he realized that there were no such leaders or communities. He returned to his coach, who encouraged him in the knowledge that God is still at work building his kingdom:

"Growth and maturity take many small steps, some twisting and turning down paths we may have never expected. New leaders often emerge slowly. Your job is not to *make* leaders; you are only responsible to pass on to faithful people that which you are learning to live out. God brings the harvest."

HELLO ... IS ANYTHING HAPPENING HERE?

There will be seasons when you will wonder if anyone is really growing and maturing in their faith and practice.

They are.

Is this really working?

It is.

As Jesus said,

> "This is what the kingdom of God is like. A man scatters seed on the ground. Night and day, whether he sleeps or gets up, the seed sprouts and grows, though he does not know how. All by itself the soil produces grain — first the stalk, then the head, then the full kernel in the head. As soon as the grain is ripe, he puts the sickle to it, because the harvest has come."[9]

> "Very truly I tell you, unless a kernel of wheat falls to the ground and dies, it remains only a single seed. But if it dies, it produces many seeds."[10]

Keep looking for your People of Peace, open your life to everyone in your extended family, make discipleship a priority and lifestyle, and give your best time and energy to those who are hungry for more. These kingdom principles are at work, and it is God who produces the harvest.

Small is Big: Who specifically are you leading and equipping, and who are you following and leaning into for your own growth and equipping? Write down the names. Ask those you are leading to share areas that they believe you can still grow in. This is humbling! But it is a necessary step in growth and models the type of leadership that honors Jesus.

Slow is Fast: Are you *accidentally* trying to raise a "crop" of leaders from within your community? More time spent with fewer leaders will ultimately put you further down the road of multiplication. Be sure that those you see as leaders know that they are being developed for leadership and multiplication. Don't assume they know. Create a plan to begin to meet with these few leaders on a regular basis for deeper development and training.

Multiplication Wins: As a part of "MAWLing" leaders in your community, encourage them to find someone to begin to pass their insights, knowledge, and skills onto next. Offer encouragement and accountability to these leaders to ensure that they follow through. Begin to pray with them for God to lead them on to multiplication and the formation of new communities.

Signpost: Passing on what you have learned to others also "reboots" your own systems as you assess how everything is going. Planning for multiplication *always* causes you to reevaluate how you are doing as a community and how effectively you are truly making disciples who can make new disciples. No one will be the perfect leader before starting a new community (you weren't either). Now is the time to be very intentionally praying for *who* you will be sending off to start new missional communities and *when* you will do so.

CHAPTER 8

THE GLORIOUS MESS

If you have ever been hiking or taken a long walk in the woods, you know how easy it can be to get lost, even when you are certain you were following the map or sticking to the trail. That phrase *"I couldn't see the forest for the trees"* becomes frighteningly real in an instant. Even with proven directions and an experienced guide, we can get off course and be far from our destination before we even know it. That's why the new satellite and aerial view maps are so helpful; you can see where you're at in relation to everything around you.

To give you a "map" and help you get a little more oriented to your surroundings, I want to share a narrative of what life for a family living on mission can look like over a typical week. Of course, there is no such thing as a typical week, but I will say that everything here is real—something experienced either in my own life or by others I know who live as an extended family. The names have been changed to protect the innocent! I've been careful not to make this too sanitized or unrealistic. Some days are packed with very obvious kingdom activity, while others feel like nothing special ... until you look back. That's often how it goes.

So here is a running journal of missional life from the perspective of a man who is married and has a few kids at different ages and stages of life. He and his family have been living as a part of a missional community for a year or two. He is learning. They are on an adventure. This may not be like your specific situation, but I hope this helps you find a few more markers along the path on your journey into the frontier of mission.

Friday 11:35pm

What a day! I could not wait to get horizontal and watch a few minutes of the *Jimmy Kimmel Live!* television program before heading off to bed. I feel *body* tired, but *soul* energized. It was a blast tonight seeing Sean and Dana, part of our MC, leading folks at the café through *Storytelling Night*. Some of the stories that people told were really nuts! But the way they led the dialogue and honored people, especially with the discussion that exploded around the *Noah's Arc* narrative, was incredible. It's amazing to see the Spirit lead people into truth through such a simple and nonthreatening time together telling stories. Several others from our MC were there too; I hope some will take a cue from this and start new story nights in the future. We'll see ...

This morning before I left for work, the kids were so funny. They were working on their list of "Who will I be a blessing to today?" Friday edition. They seem to argue a lot about who and what, but they laugh a lot too. It seems that this is becoming a rhythm to our day ... well, *most* days. We prayed with them before they left for the school bus, and now the list is displayed in anticipation on the refrigerator:

> Mom—Send a note encouraging Tiff who is sick
> Dad—Drop off the lawnmower for Nick after work
> Molly—Offer to pay for the student retreat for Sara
> Teddy—Mow the lawn for Nick and Old Man Jansen
> Chase—Tell my teacher Ms. Linda how much she helps me

Molly is now a freshman in college—whoa! Teddy is loving the ninth grade, and Chase is tolerating fourth grade. Two out of three ain't bad ... I have great kids, Lord!

I am sensing that Tony, a friend at work, may be a *person of peace* in my life. He is such a cool guy and is always asking me questions about my past, my marriage, why I do certain things—or don't. And he's always offering to help me out with whatever I happen to mention I've got to do, or something that's happening in our MC. I'm stoked that he is coming with us to serve at the park tomorrow. We can use the help!

I am intrigued by the conversation I had with Nick after work today. He was grateful that we were helping him with his lawn and all the yard work, but he was more interested in how Teddy, our middle-schooler, would be willing to help *and* have such a great attitude about all of it. The last six weeks since his surgery have been rough on him, and while he accepts our help, I can tell that he is feeling like a burden. Teddy told him today, "It's not that we *have* to help mow your lawn, Nick; it doesn't look that bad. But we *get* to. It's our pleasure!"

Nick was blown away by that and continues to promise to "pay us back somehow." We told him we were both hoping for new Corvettes!

Sherry is the best wife a guy could ever have. I don't know how we would live our lives like this on mission without her. Her growing flexibility when it comes to our family's schedule is awesome. She has always been great at having people over and hospitality, but now that she's not so worried about keeping a perfect house, it seems like she's having a lot more fun and everyone else is more relaxed around our place. There are definitely fewer leftovers in the fridge these days—mostly because Molly seems to bring new friends over for dinner most nights.

I feel as if our "family" is growing up, in, and out a lot quicker these days!

I should sleep. Tomorrow will be cool, but busy ...

Saturday night around midnight

My buddy Bob is always the first to arrive. Again today he grabbed a bunch of our younger folks and went over to set things up ... *way* before the rest of us arrived. Every few months we work with our city officials to identify some park or other part of the city that needs some love and attention. Today we earned our stripes by pulling a record number of weeds from Center Park and spreading out literally *tons* of mulch. These projects, which we call *Sacred Space,* save the city a few bucks, but more than that, it has given us the opportunity to invite lots of friends and neighbors to join us as we live as a blessing to others. We don't always point this out to them right away, but it *always* seems to come up in conversation when the question of "why do you all do this stuff?" comes up.

I was able to make some great observations today about a couple of the leaders I am developing in our MC. It is surprising to see how hard some work at the *task* while others work hard at the *mission*. The mission is always about the people ... always about discipling others to the truth in new areas of life. They're really starting to get this. Cool!

Sherry and a few others from our MC shot out a little early from the project to set up a barbecue lunch at our house. When we finished at the park, around half of our MC and a few others enjoyed a simple, and much appreciated, meal together. Terry and Taylor (neighbors who came to help) seem to really be "leaning in" to relationship lately. They were so happy to do all this with us: they wore their fresh blisters as badges of honor!

After the community helped clean up from lunch, I managed to sneak in a little reading (mostly napping). Yes! The kids who were home seemed glued to their smartphones anyway ...

Tonight Molly and a couple of her college friends came over to watch the basketball game on television and finish off the leftovers from the BBQ. My job was to keep the mountains of fresh popcorn coming. Sherry bugged out and went upstairs early to read, rest, take a bubble bath, whatever she does when we watch sports. Good for her.

When I came up to bed myself, Sherry was still awake. She asked if we could pray together for Terry and Taylor. *"Father, thank you for loving us so well. Thanks for this awesome day to serve you, and thanks for Terry and Taylor becoming a part of this family—your family. Will you show us how to pass on to them the love you have shown us? We ask you to continue to stir up questions and desires in their hearts! Amen and good night."*

Sunday 2:30pm after the gathering

Crazy! Last night my work buddy Tony texted me saying he wanted to go do "the church thing" with me this morning. So he joined us with a few folks from the MC who decided to go to our church gathering together. He took a lot of notes and surprised me again, saying he wanted to ask me a few questions later …

A few others from our MC were here too, but dispersed into various serving jobs among the younger kids and nursery duty. We all had lunch at the Salad & Soup Shop after the gathering. I think Tony likes being around some of the single gals in our group! I can't wait to see what questions he has … I have a few of my own.

Sunday 9:50pm

I was catching a nap snuggled on the couch with Sherry at around 4:30 when the phone rang. It was Old Man Jansen calling to tell us his toilet had sprung a leak and he didn't know what to do. I took the boys and Sean from our MC over there (overkill), and we fixed it in no time (well, after two trips to the Home Depot). Mr. Jansen insisted that he order pizzas and feed us before we all left. He told us his entire life story starting back from his childhood. My boys asked him all sorts of questions — which only served to throw fuel on his fire. He loved it! (So did we.)

We need to start inviting this guy over for dinner and other MC stuff. I think he is super-ready in need of a family and community.

When I got home, Sherry was in a "spiritual discussion" with Molly and a couple of her friends from her Psychology class, discussing "free will and the human condition" or something like that. They were deep into debating why the world is so messed up. They pulled me into the discussion at one point, and I had the opportunity to tell a small portion of the Story as part of my contribution. Molly's friends really related to that and started kicking around the idea of going through the entire Story-formed Way together with a couple others from their class ... purely as an "academic exercise," some of them suggested.

More to pray about!

Monday

(A holiday and day off from "work" ... it's dark now.)

Holidays are the best ... and busiest days of the year. What killer opportunities to lean into the celebrations of our culture. I keep telling our MC that these days are "low-hanging fruit"!

Today we had a neighborhood cookout and watermelon-eating contest. A tradition we've started that gets bigger and bigger each year. Normally Sherry meets on Monday morning with a few other moms and a single gal from our MC for their DNA group, but this morning she asked them all to come over to our place to help her set up for the day.

Two couples that we have invited a MILLION times to our parties, cookouts, etc., showed up for the first time. They were super apologetic and stayed until the very end, thanking us repeatedly and asking if they could host something like this for the neighborhood soon ... *if* we would help them. Of course ... you *get* to!

Our son Teddy's girlfriend and her parents came today too. They are part of a church in the neighborhood, but asked a lot of questions about our missional community. They said they keep hearing from others in the neighborhood about us and the MC and have always wanted to be a part of something like this ...

"There has to be more to this Christian thing than just a couple hours each week, right?!"

Being a school day tomorrow, most folks left by seven o'clock. Everyone helped clean up and put the yard and house back together, so Sherry and I were able to take a walk along the riverfront with Teddy, Chase, and another family that we just met today. They recently moved to our neighborhood and are looking for "a church or something." Their last experience left them dry and tired, and they're thinking they need to find a community to be with.

We might be able to help them out with this ...

Tuesday 9:30am

I got to work late today because I needed to help Chase set up his project for the science fair at school. I jumped in on this so that Sherry could watch one of our neighbor's kids; her sitter bailed at the last minute and she had an important job interview. Sherry's been doing Sharonda's laundry for her for the past few months and picking up slack since her husband left her and the kids. They have become part of our extended family. They are super-needy and we're glad for both the help our community offers *and* the opportunity for service that Sharonda and the kids give us. Helping them is teaching us to have the heart of Jesus while showing his heart to her. It's cool how that works.

Tuesday 9:30pm

This day flew by!

Tony, my buddy at work, asked me more about God today — what I believed and some of the questions he had from Sunday. He's been around our house a lot lately, seeing and experiencing what our family is like. He knows we're all about Jesus and seems drawn to our community and what we're doing.

I told him I best understood my faith from learning the story found in the Bible and living it out tangibly with others. My faith is not a set of religious dos and don'ts that I've somehow espoused, or something that I try hard at keeping and feel crummy when I don't. He said he would love to hear this "story of God" sometime if there was ever an opportunity. I assured him there would be ... a few of us were thinking of starting to have dinner together once a week and start going through the Story.

Sherry took some extra brownies she baked to a neighbor across the street and ended up getting into a cool conversation about marriage. She explained that marriage was given as a picture of what God is like. When we live in light of God's plans for marriage, we see he is good, loving, and forgiving. When we don't, it reminds us of how much we really need him in our lives.

We had a quiet dinner at home tonight. Nice!

Sherry and I listened to the kids share how their "blessings" for the day had gone, and then we caught up on our favorite

TV shows a little. Teddy tried to get out of studying for an exam he has tomorrow … sorry, pal!

Wednesday

I really got a kick out of today's "blessings list":

> Who will I be a blessing to today?—Wednesday
>
> Mom—Loan Sharonda my car today while hers is in the shop
> Dad—Give Tony that book he was asking about
> Molly—Take Mom to Starbucks so she can have a pumpkin latte
> Teddy—Stick around after school to help set up the room for PTA
> Chase—Tell my teacher Ms. Linda she's pretty hot

I'm noticing a trend here with Chase wanting to bless his teacher Ms. Linda. I'll have to talk to him about this one … Ha!

Sherry took advantage of not having a car today and organized a walk in the park with a few of the ladies from the neighborhood. She said that nothing "heavy" was discussed, but they had agreed that they all needed to do this more often and swapped email addresses so they could make good on this promise.

Molly showed up, as planned, and took her mother out for a pumpkin latte. *They* in fact *did* have a "heavy" conversation. About boys, one in particular, and Molly's growing attraction to this young man. He is a very casual Christian, and she is not sure how to respond to his advances toward her in the relationship. Sherry listened mostly, and then suggested that Molly start having this guy hang around our community more frequently and meet a few of her "brothers" … let them do some of the hard work of vetting this one. Molly liked that idea.

This evening we went to another couple's house for "family dinner night" with our entire MC. It was a fun night. We discussed our plans for starting to go through the Story-formed Way in a few weeks and prayed, "What next, Lord?" for all of our People of Peace. Before leaving, I promised to have coffee next week with a new guy, Nick, and talk about his job future with him. I am going to bring Bob with me from the MC because he is younger and just learning how to apply the gospel to his own future career, and he wants to learn how to help others do the same.

I think Bob is going to lead his own MC in the near future. I've told him this, and he is really stepping up to new areas of leadership and helping others grow in their gospel fluency. He is definitely yeast in the dough!

Thursday 6:00am

Up and out the door early today ... I really love these times with my DNA group. This hour or so we spend over breakfast each week is often the richest, meatiest time we'll spend together. I'm amazed at the trust that the three of us have built and how it has allowed us to go so much deeper into the real "stuff of life" with one another. We all have so much farther to go ... Last week when we met, we almost forgot to pay our server—time had slipped away (again) and we all left encouraged, but super late for work!

Thursday 10:30pm

I was able to get home early today, which was awesome, since there was a soccer game for Chase at four o'clock. Several of the folks in our MC showed up to cheer their heads off and help provide drinks and snacks for the whole team. The other parents love that we do this every game, but are still a little perplexed as to why Chase has such a large, generous family ... We can't wait to get the opportunity to tell them more.

Chase and I grabbed some fast food on the way home afterward. Tonight is Game Night at our place with Molly's roommates from college and a couple other gals from her volleyball team. It followed a dinner that all the girls made together, getting cooking tips from Sherry along the way. Lots of fun, and a great meal of pork tenderloin with special bacon-and-cream mashed potatoes.

Wow! It gets loud in there ... but since my boy Teddy and I play basketball with guys at the YMCA most weeks on Thursday nights, we escaped the pandemonium.

When we got home, Molly rushed up excitedly to tell me that some of the girls from her team have also agreed to start going through the Story together. She is a little scared to lead in this, but I reminded her that she has grown up in the Story and has been a part of taking others through this experience a zillion times.

She said, *"I know ... but always with you and Mom and a whole bunch of people in our MC ..."*

I hugged her and told her, "Sweetie, you'll do this in community too. You already have a big group that wants to do this with you, and God has placed you in a huge family that is here to help."

It was a good day, Lord!

FINDING YOUR WAY

Again, I realize this may not be the exact stage of life or the situation you find yourself in right now, but I hope it has helped you see the normalcy of a life lived as an extended family on mission. Some days are busier than others, and some things are organized, while others are very organic. Not everything happens as quickly as or in the way we want it to. People drop off the radar and out of community. This is messy stuff! On this journey, you must trust that God is filling your lives with opportunities for discipleship and kingdom expansion every day. Some you will notice; others you may not.

If you are reading this and thinking, *"Whoa! That's a lot of stuff ... I'm way too busy for that...,"* I have two suggestions for you. First, go back over the rhythms we covered in Chapter 6 and notice how many of these fall under the normal patterns of life. The difference is that they are being "recycled" with a new *intention* toward discipleship and the gospel. But no extra time is required.

Second, remember that there are really only two or three interactions with the MC during this week that fall outside these normal daily and weekly rhythms. But you find a sweet spot to your schedule when these few organized activities pave the way for all the rest of discipleship to naturally occur. I also hope you see that one of the takeaways from this family's schedule is that everything is moving outward with regard to its activities, responsibilities, and relationships. Growth is happening as the family includes others, more and more frequently, into the mix. Treating everyone like family.

Above all, it's a matter of gospel intentionality.

Small is Big: Set aside an hour or so *this* week to create a calendar that blocks out very specifically the organized aspects of your life on mission. This may not represent what you're currently doing, but should be the goal with which you strive to get in line. The more intentional we are about things like meals with persons of peace, time with leaders, serving times, and our own development, etc., the greater momentum and consistency on mission we will experience. This small exercise will have great impact on your life.

Slow is Fast: Did this chapter give you any specific ideas for organized or organic interactions that you can incorporate immediately? What are they? Who else will you need to include before implementing? How is your MC doing at regularly serving others as a way of being a blessing, and what is next for you?

Multiplication Wins: Hopefully you're seeing how normal life can involve the discipleship and development of leaders as long as you *choose* to include them in the things you do. What are one or two *new* daily activities you can invite leaders to join you in as a part of the mission and their leadership development? Challenge your leaders to do the same things with those they are developing. Think about the "4 Gen Explosion" from the previous chapter.

Signpost: As you move further down the path into this life on mission, your family and community will continue to evolve and develop their own patterns as you grow in greater gospel intentionality. You're seeing that this is a messy process. Things come up that you never could have planned, and they are very often the *best* occasion for discipleship that could be hoped for. Look to see all of life as an ongoing opportunity to help others move from unbelief to belief. At this point you are realizing in greater ways the need to rely on the Holy Spirit for all of this!

CHAPTER 9

SOMETIMES SUNDAY HAPPENS

It didn't happen every year, but when it did, it was awesome. From as far back as I can remember, my Polish relatives would come together for huge family reunions. Usually it would happen every other year or so, but regardless of the frequency, these were epic events. We would all get back together as one big family, and it was as if no time had passed. Everyone was glad to be together and picked up the conversations (or feuds) right where we had left off.

I remember running into people I knew from school or my bowling league, only to find out that they were in fact a "cousin of a cousin" and we had never known about the connection. It was great to realize that I was a part of a much larger network of relatives — a family spread out all over town. There were grandparents and great-grandparents, a million aunts and uncles, cousins, new babies, games, and ... FOOD!

If you wanted to learn how to play horseshoes, you would learn from the best—Uncle Walter and Little John. These guys crushed everyone and then gloated about it. My father could never beat either of them, but he tried nonetheless. If you wanted to learn how to make the best Polish foods, after sampling an endless variety, you could get recipes and tips from all the aunts and cousins. Passing on the traditions, passing on the goodness and love.

These celebrations were filled with stories we had never heard before—or were tired of hearing—yet they touched us in deep ways. They connected us to our traditions and reminded us of who we were, who I still am today. They formed my identity and our identity as a family. These times connected our younger family members to older ones, and being together made us grateful and excited to be a part of this growing family.

It was imperfect, for sure, but it was *our* family.

A COMMUNITY GATHERED

Whenever we come together as the church, this is what we're experiencing too: a family reunion. Our gatherings are times filled with brothers, sisters, and spiritual parents all getting together, not out of compulsion or duty, but from a desire to bond, grow, and show love for one another. Some of you may have started on this journey of living as a family on mission with the goal of planting a new church in your city. Others may have experienced growth and multiplication in your MC and now seek the benefits that can be gained when the larger family comes back together with all their different gifts, perspectives, and experiences.

Not everyone who reads this book will want to see their MC grow into a new, public gathering akin to a church "service." You might even be asking the question, "Do we *need* to have larger gatherings or bring all of our missional communities together?"

No. But you *get* to.

I sincerely believe that there are great biblical, historical, and pragmatic reasons to gather together as the larger body of Christ ... when the timing is right. And in appropriate ways that foster, rather than hinder, the mission of making disciples. I have found on numerous occasions that as our own MC has multiplied, and then in turn the new MCs have multiplied again, there is a real and natural desire for everyone to want to be together, to see those brothers and sisters whom we have discipled and sent, to hear their stories and share ours. We missed the unique gifts and perspectives of the others, so we began planning how and when we could start "gathering up the family" to remember God's goodness to us, pray for one another, and learn forward. And we found that it could happen on Sunday ... Tuesday ... or any other day of the week.

Before long, by God's grace, you may find yourself in a similar situation, with similar needs and desires for your community. But don't start off by thinking that the goal here is to get a *big ol' church service* going with all of the programs and challenges of space, money, and staffing. Rather, think of it more as a celebration or a family reunion, where everyone brings something to share, telling their stories of what God is doing in their lives and being encouraged and equipped for mission in the rest of their normal life rhythms. At times, the things you do together may resemble some of the stuff you have experienced or heard about churches doing in the past, but it's important to be sure you know *why* you're doing what you do when you gather, and what the overall goals for those times together should be.

WHO DOES WHAT?

The apostle Paul, who arguably started the majority of the churches we read about in the New Testament, tells us in 1 Corinthians 14 what it should be like when we gather together as the church. Note that he is *not* saying that this is the only way this works or that it only happens at a formal church service or in a church building, as some have tried to argue. Paul says that when a larger group of saints gathers, possibly from multiple *oikos,* and comes together as God's family, there is a certain flavor to their gathering. I love the way Eugene Peterson translates this (emphasis mine):

> So here's what I want you to do. When you gather for worship, *each one of you* be prepared with something that will be useful for all: Sing a hymn, teach a lesson, tell a story, lead a prayer, provide an insight. If prayers are offered in tongues, two or three's the limit, and then only if someone is present who can interpret what you're saying. Otherwise, keep it between God and yourself. And no more than two or three speakers at a meeting, with the rest of you listening and taking it to heart. Take your turn, *no one person taking over.* Then each speaker gets a chance to say something special from God, and you all learn from each other. If you choose to speak, you're also responsible for how and when you speak. When we worship the right way, God doesn't stir us up into confusion; he brings us into harmony. *This goes for all the churches — no exceptions.*[1]

You will notice here that there are a lot of different things going on and everyone is invited into the mix. Jesus speaks

"So often the church service that we quietly sit through every Sunday, year after year, actually hinders spiritual transformation. It does so because (1) it encourages passivity, (2) it limits functioning, and (3) it implies that putting in one hour per week is the key to the victorious Christian life."

—FRANK VIOLA AND GEORGE BARNA[2]

by his Spirit to and through everyone who is submitted to him. This community aspect of our being together is vital to the overall health, maturity, and witness of the church in any context.

Everyone is needed. Everyone is important.

If, when you gather your MCs together, just a few special people do everything, you tear down what's been seeded into your community life where everyone has a role and is a vital part of the body of Christ. However, as larger gatherings begin to take place, you will need to be sure that the extended church family understands that the brothers or sisters with more mature and developed skills (i.e., those that are appropriate and helpful for these larger gatherings) may share their gifts more frequently and in more noticeable ways. They are modeling something for everyone. Also, the community should begin to see these same mature saints equipping others and seeding multiplication and growth into every aspect of these gathered times. This is part of our discipleship too.

A REMINDER AND A DEMONSTRATION

So why do we gather? Is a gathering of the church (people) meant to be a gathering of individuals who come to worship and learn individually while occupying the same room, or, like the rest of their life in Christ, is the gathering of the saints a communal experience of the gospel that is filled up and enriched as we interact with one another, the Word of God, and the Holy Spirit? If you vote for the second option (as I would), then I wonder why so much of what happens at traditional corporate gatherings is individually focused in message (personal renewal) and limited participation (I listen; one person does all the talking), and then we all leave and go back to our respective "corners" alone? The church is a family *wherever* it is. I have learned that our corporate gatherings should not look all that different from our life together in community. These times should be an extension of our life as a family, not something unique and different.

These times should serve as both a *reminder* and a *demonstration*.

Our theology (who God is and how he acts in the world) informs and shapes our missiology (what God is doing in the world, his mission), and our missiology shapes and determines our ecclesiology (how we act and live together) as the church.

God commanded Israel, his earthly family, to institute several festivals and feasts throughout the year. These celebrations all served both as a reminder of who God is and what he is like (theology) and as a demonstration of how the Israelites were to live in relationship to God and others throughout the rest of the year (ecclesiology), not just during the festivals. They also demonstrated to a watching world, the nations that interacted with the Jews, who their God was and his desires for all people (mission).

For instance, Israel's third annual celebration is called the feast of firstfruits,[3] and it served to remind the people that God is a consistent and generous provider. Therefore they could count on God throughout the year and, in turn, live generously in light of his great provision. The feast reminded them of the truth and was a demonstration of how they would *get* to live all year. Do you see how that works? It's really a picture of the gospel. Each of the Jewish festivals followed this pattern.

When Jesus ate his last meal with his disciples, it was in commemoration of another of these celebrations: the Passover. This celebration was a reminder of how God had rescued Israel from slavery and delivered them into freedom and blessing. Their continued celebration of the original Passover,[4] an event that originally happened back in Egypt hundreds of years earlier, was now to be a reminder of God's freedom and a demonstration of how the Israelites could continue to live free because of who God is and what he had done. When Jesus served his disciples the bread and invited them to drink from the cup, he connected the dots for them to a new covenant, a more complete and final freedom that he was offering to them. He told them to continue doing this together often, until he would come back to party with them again.

The apostle Paul, when teaching those in the early church how to gather together and understand the great significance in doing this, always structured the gathering times around a meal. It was one meal in particular — the meal Jesus told his followers to celebrate.

> For I received from the Lord what I also passed on to you: The Lord Jesus, on the night he was betrayed, took bread, and when he had given thanks, he broke it and said, "This is my body, which is for you; do this in remembrance of me." In the

same way, after supper he took the cup, saying, "This cup is the new covenant in my blood; do this, whenever you drink it, in remembrance of me." For whenever you eat this bread and drink this cup, you proclaim the Lord's death until he comes.[5]

You will notice that twice Paul says to do this as a way of being reminded of what Jesus has done for us through his life, death, and resurrection. We celebrate the meal so we don't forget it! This meal was called the *agape feast* by the early Christians, and it demonstrated their belief in the gospel while putting it on display for all who joined them in their celebrations and gatherings.

It worked this way for Israel, it worked this way with Jesus, and it continued on with God's family, the church. I believe that we need to evaluate how and why we gather, in all sizes and configurations, through these same two perspectives of *reminder* and *demonstration*.

Is everything we're doing reminding us of who God is and what he has accomplished while also demonstrating how we should live together in culture throughout all of life, every day? If we are doing something based on tradition alone or personal preference and it does not serve these twin purposes, I suggest that it needs to be questioned as to how helpful it really is in accomplishing the mission of making disciples who make disciples.

> Then some Pharisees and teachers of the law came to Jesus from Jerusalem and asked, "Why do your disciples break the tradition of the elders? . . ."
>
> Jesus replied, "And why do you break the command of God for the sake of your tradition?"[6]

Think about how your gatherings can help aid in the accomplishment of the mission. How can the elements of your gathered times reinforce your gospel identity and accurately represent what God is like? Can the brothers and sisters easily transfer what they see, hear, learn, and experience in these gathered times — private or public — into the regular flow and rhythms of life?

THE CELEBRATION CONTINUES

When trying to determine the types of specific activities and practices you should include in a larger gathering, ask yourself, "What would a big, healthy family that has God as their Daddy and Jesus as their Brother do when they get together?" Seriously! Think about that together as a community of multiple communities, and I believe you will find your answer. Here are some things we have learned:

Food: Healthy families eat together — abundantly, extravagantly. Bring your best dishes, your favorite meals and drinks, to share with your brothers and sisters. If Jesus were there (and he is, though not physically), you would not stop on the way for a bucket of fried chicken or bring a bag of tortilla chips and a jar of salsa. Like Jesus, who made the better wine at a wedding in Cana, bring your very best in all that you do for your family. This is a display of our belief that God gave his best when he sent us Jesus.

Teaching: It often proves beneficial during these gathered times to include some type of teaching or devotional thoughts that have been determined by the leaders of the various missional communities to be profitable for making disciples. Often someone will teach or lead a time in the Word, using dialogue as a way of processing the learning time with everyone. Be sure that the things being taught can be reproduced in the lives and practice of everyone. Topics for teaching and discussion should not be chosen randomly, but should address felt needs for the overall community at that time.

Worship: People who as Christians have participated in "church services" before, or frequently in their past, often consider *worship* to be a time of singing. And it can be. But worship is an attitude of the heart that can and does include reading Scripture out loud, poetry, artwork, dance, prayer, a special meal together, or unique talents and abilities offered to God as a way of expressing his *worth-ship*. Singing together is great, when appropriate and not forced, but we can express a heart of worship together in many ways.

Filter your ideas through the principles of "a reminder and a demonstration" as you craft your times together. Let everything you do as the gathered church serve to model how you would articulate and live out the gospel in all of life. Make room for the kids to participate in meaningful ways, and leave space for spontaneous feedback, praise, and stories of how God is at work in your MCs or family.

It is also important to keep multiplication in mind in all that you do. Be sure to plan your gatherings in ways that are simple, low cost, and reproducible as the community continues to expand and grow. Others will, in faith, soon be leading new, regathered communities, and you do not want to set the bar at a level where people feel that they have to perform or "freak out" over replicating what they have experienced in the past.

BE THE CHURCH

The church is and has always been people. Our identity is found in Christ, not the frequency or size of our gatherings.

> *"There is no distinction in the New Testament between priests and laity, the sacred and the secular, the religious and the everyday."*
>
> —MICHAEL FROST AND ALAN HIRSCH[7]

Therefore, we are no more or no less "the church" if we gather outside of our normal MC rhythms with other Christians weekly, than if we do it monthly or ... whenever. There is not a "forsaking of the assembling of ourselves together"[8] if you are living your lives as a gospel-centered community on mission, together an extension of God's family. Larger *congregations* serve the movement and facilitate multiplication of disciples, but do not define us as the church.

Being the church is part of our identity as a family of God living on his mission. The church is people, not buildings and services. We are not *really* a church just because we have a building of our own to start public gatherings. However, we are collectively more mature and gifted than any one of us alone. There are far greater and more mature gifts present in a *congregation* of people than in a single MC. God has promised to give us all that we need to be equipped for ministry, obtain unity in our faith, and reach maturity,[9] but he has not promised that every gift will be present in *each* MC alone. Jesus prayed that we would work *together* in love and unity.[10]

This is why I am an advocate for MCs working collectively as connected and networked congregations, sharing leadership and resources. We have so much more together than apart. We can grow and multiply at a far greater pace when we employ all of the gifts that God has poured into our communities.

For leaders to be humbly working together and submitting to one another's gifts is crucial because it reminds us of our needs. And it reminds us of how our King meets our needs. It is a display of the humility Jesus showed as he submitted to his Father, and it demonstrates that his Spirit—the same Spirit who led and empowered the early church on mission—leads and lives in us too.

WHEN TO BEGIN?

How soon should leaders begin to have more public, or even private, larger gatherings that include multiple missional communities? The answer: when it serves the mission.

Don't rush to it or fear it.

I know several communities that began to have larger gatherings once they multiplied to three or four MCs or they desired to gather together with other MCs from their city or region. At first they met once a month for a meal and some equipping and prayer together. They added or subtracted the frequency of these gatherings as needed to best match the rhythms of the season or school year within their culture. These times together evolved as the community did. In the same way that any family grows and matures, so did their needs and functions over time.

Be flexible. And most of all, ask the Holy Spirit to guide you.

SOMETIMES SUNDAY HAPPENS TOO SOON

A few years ago, while Soma Communities was helping plant new churches in Tacoma, we sent off three different groups of missional communities that had grown and multiplied to "go and be" under their own leadership. Each of the three leadership teams almost immediately started trying to pull off "Sunday services" for their regathered communities. It turns out, however, that this was a mistake.

When I would visit with each of these groups of leaders, it seemed that much — or most — of their time was spent talking about and critiquing last weekend's large gathering or planning the next one. Less and less of their time was spent working through and praying about individual people or their community health. They had begun losing their focus on discipleship and leadership development within the MCs themselves. Growth in these communities had flattened out, and in some cases, folks were leaving the community altogether.

Some of us who were elders within the larger body noticed this trend and offered a solution. We asked them, "What would you think about continuing to lead your missional communities as a team, without having to worry for a while about having to put together a larger combined gathering?" All three of the teams immediately declared, "That would be awesome! Then we could get back to making disciples and developing our leaders more effectively." So for a while that's what they did. Those who wanted to could come to one of the other weekend gatherings that were happening in town, where they could hear the Word taught and participate in the larger expression of our church community. But in the rhythms of the rest of their week, things went back to "normal," with the leaders' time and best energy and efforts directed to discipleship. Things immediately began to grow and expand again. We learned a valuable lesson from this experience.

The mission of the church is discipleship, *not* creating church services.

While larger gatherings *can* be effective in helping us grow as the church, they can also become distractions. We've got to keep the mission clear.

ONE HAPPY FAMILY

On more than one occasion I have seen churches that started out as a single missional community and then, after multiplying into several communities, began having combined public gatherings. But over time as things progressed, the growing "congregation" unintentionally formed into two groups of people — two different "bodies," if you will.

There were those who still saw their MC as their primary expression and engagement as the church, while participating in the larger gatherings when they could and when it didn't interfere with other aspects of their life on mission. And there were others who came and found the community via the Sunday gathering and staunchly preferred this form of church, coming primarily to hear the preaching and to hang out with other Christians. They treated community life as optional or saw it as a weekly small group meeting to be fit into *their* schedules when convenient.

I discussed this challenge with a trusted friend and partner in mission, Seth McBee, and we came up with several suggestions to help people either move *in* or move *on*:

- Make it hard to feel comfortable being in the gathering for very long without being part of a missional community.

- Have a clearly defined invitation and pathway to community, coupled with a growing challenge.

- Be sure if someone expresses interest in finding a community to be a part of that they are followed up on thoroughly and do not fall through the cracks.

- Make sure to give MC leaders plenty of time to tell stories about new life and mission during the gatherings.

- Make community-wide announcements and training opportunities known through your MC life and interactions instead of at the gatherings. Let people know this is how communication flows in this family.

- Carefully select what will be taught or "preached" at a gathering, ensuring that it always catalyzes mission and helps grow everyone in gospel fluency.

- Be sure that everyone knows that "counseling" and soul care happen primarily in community, not one-to-one in an office with a professional.

- Communicate that all benevolence and financial care happen in and through life in an MC.

This is one more thing to watch for as you add new ports of entry into the life of Jesus. There will be people who first find you as a community via your larger or more public gatherings. It is imperative that they know the family story and are clear that the two hours spent together this way is just that: two hours within a much larger framework and rhythm of a large family on mission.

UNCHURCHED, DECHURCHED, OR DISINTERESTED

When I was a young father, our family got a puppy from an animal shelter, one of those places that is loud and smelly and loves any and every lost or forsaken pet there is. Another family had previously owned this dog, and when we got it home, we noticed that whenever we would reach down to pet the little fella, he would shrink back into a ball on the floor in fear. It seemed as if he must have been abused for so long that he didn't know how to receive love.

There are people like that too. They're all around us.

Some of them have been hurt in relationships, by neglectful parents or at the hands of selfish leaders in their life. And there are some who have had bad experiences with the church. Many people will say they are "done with religion." They have wounds and perceived problems with the church, or they fear additional abuse by anyone they see as an authority figure. Any opportunity we can give them to engage with God's people in a way that makes them able to reapproach our Father's love is a good thing.

The gospel moves at the speed of trust.

Community expands along the lines of friendships and family.

Finally, I want to say that it is important that we not disdain any particular form or size of gathering together. There are many ways to gather together and celebrate Jesus. Not everyone will see it the way we do or prefer things the same way. Rejoice wherever the gospel is proclaimed. Celebrate when saints are equipped and empowered to make disciples. Be delighted when any part of the Family provides shelter from the storm for those who are far from the Kingdom and our great King, Jesus!

Small is Big: A church is not defined by its larger gathering times. And it is hard to start a "new church" by thinking primarily about the things and practices you *don't* want to do or be about. Discuss with your missional community the types of interactions and activities that you believe would be beneficial and propel your people further into the mission of making disciples if you were to gather together in larger community times, perhaps even publicly.

Slow is Fast: Have you multiplied and sent out parts of your extended family to start new missional communities? Are there others in your city or region who have done the same? Organize a monthly meeting of leaders to discuss the possibilities of gathering, training, and equipping together for the sake of the mission in your area. Don't let tradition or denominational lines get in your way.

Multiplication Wins: I want to strongly encourage you to spend some time looking into and learning from the community that is the GCM Collective. I and others help lead this ministry that is designed to help new missional communities form and multiply with the audacious, God-breathed goal of seeing one MC per one thousand people in every city. We're here to help. Find us at www.gcmcollective.org.

Signpost: You may be one or two years into the journey at this point. You have learned a lot, but have also come to see that there is so much more to learn! For all of the reasons given above, it may be time to consider next steps together as a larger, re-congregated community. Perhaps that was your goal all along.

Wherever you're at and whatever you're thinking, let the Holy Spirit be your strength, wisdom, and primary advisor as you continue on the greatest adventure that man has ever known! Go be the church.

CONCLUSION:
A KINGDOM
MOVEMENT

One of the hardest things about writing this book has been deciding what to leave out. There is no way to give you everything a person might need to know, so I'm just hitting the tip of the missional iceberg here. There are learnings and experiences I would love to share with you if only there were more space and time to do so. Some of you might have more questions now than when you began reading! Keep going; keep seeking answers. Don't fear failure, but rather *suck forward*. You will not do any of this perfectly at first, but even if you suck at it, if you learn and continue on, then you will not have failed.

That's life as a disciple.

G. K. Chesterton has been quoted as saying, *"If a thing is worth doing, it is worth doing badly."*[1] To that I would add: *"... at first."* Many times we fail to begin because we falsely believe that we must know how to make *every* step perfectly *before* we start. We want to guarantee victory and ensure our own glory before we strike out and take a risk. But this is just a lack of faith, and it betrays our self-centeredness at the core.

Suck forward, trust God. You only need to ask, know, and obey....

"What next, Lord?"

In Appendix A you will find a timeline titled "*By the Numbers*" that integrates everything you have read here into a possible timeline showing what, when, and how long all of this might take. Along with the timeline, in Appendix B I share something called "*The Discipleship Environment of Jesus.*" It's a helpful framework you can use to remind yourself of how Jesus made disciples and how to keep focused on what's important. I hope you'll find both of these tools useful.

NOW WHAT?

Some of you, after reading this book, may be persuaded that *none* of this is for you. I am sorry. I don't know what to say. I really don't. I am personally convinced and convicted that this is a biblical model for how we are to live and follow Jesus' command to make disciples.

On the other hand, hopefully many of you are ready to begin this life that God created you to live. In fact, you may have already begun this journey and are feeling called to increase your leadership beyond your extended family and missional community. God is guiding and shaping you for greater things to come someday.

That day may be today.

More than likely God is building you into part of a team—a family—that he is preparing for the next season of growth and multiplication. Continue to let the Holy Spirit disciple you toward all God has for your life and his glory. If you are committed to this process and want to be fully trained and coached by practitioners over a two-year period, there are opportunities for you to learn. We will walk with you from the first baby steps up through multiplication. You can learn more about this and find out how to participate by visiting launch.3dmovements.com.

THE KINGDOM IS AT HAND

My hope is that you have come to see that the missional life isn't just a matter of a new method of discipleship. It's not just about planting more churches. The truth is that one-to-one discipleship hasn't worked all that great, at least not when it comes to multiplying movements. And planting churches by addition isn't filling our growing cities with the gospel at a rate fast enough to meet the need. I am convinced that it is time for us to work together across cities and regions to see rapid multiplication of gospel-centered communities living on mission. The sheer amount of leadership gifts and human and tangible resources that can (and should) be pooled together in a city for the sake of the Kingdom is staggering compared to what can be offered individually.

For the last few years, with my being the director of the GCM Collective, we have helped lead others to start missional communities around the world, all with the focus of working together to reach their cities and their region with the good news. It starts by working with everyone you know who is willing to live a lifestyle of discipleship, laying down your worries about "Where will they attend on Sunday?" or "Who will get their offerings?" and moving toward seeing your brothers and sisters as your spiritual family. It's time that we extend our Father's family out to every man, woman, and child in our cities.

Will you be part of this powerful movement of the gospel, or will you add this book to the stack of books you've read full of "good ideas" and move on to something else?

This is a journey, and together we hope to see one missional community for every one thousand people in your city. Please believe that God can do this! It doesn't require large, formal structures or lots of money. The kingdom principles are what make it work. Small is big. Slow is fast. And multiplication wins. We see this happening in many cities already.

Can you imagine living in a city or township of twelve thousand people, and someday helping to see twelve missional communities emerge? What about a city of thirty or even fifty thousand? Do you believe that over time, as you work toward multiplication, God could bless your city with thirty or fifty missional communities over the next five to ten years? We can already see this happening in many places.

To hear more of my own stories and insights as they unfold, follow me on Twitter @CaesarKal. I also invite you to dig deep into the resources available to you at www.gcmcollective.org. You will also find the largest networked community of missional people and leaders in the world there. They are your family, and they want to help. Ask them! You are not expected to "save your city," but you have been commissioned to give your life as a part of a family of missionary servants, who are sent as disciples who make disciples to fill the world with

God's glory. This is not an alternative program of the church. This is God's mission.

And God always fulfills what he has commanded.

APPENDIX A

BY THE NUMBERS

Since you've made it this far in the book and are committed to a lifestyle of discipleship, starting a missional community and/or planting a church, the following assumes you are serious about this! This potential timeline is not meant to perfectly fit your lives, schedule, and pace, but rather to give you an idea of how things can and have progressed for me and others who live as extended families—missional communities—together. I know you will still have many, many more questions after reading through this, but you'll have to dig into the resources referenced in Appendix C, re-read certain chapters, and seek the guidance and wisdom of the Holy Spirit at every step of this journey if you are to succeed.

This is not everything you will ever do together as an MC (missional community). There will be the need for additional times of Bible study and prayer together, meals, retreats, parties, and serving opportunities that you'll need to integrate into this as you go. Try not to think of everything as perfectly linear—moving from one step to another—but more like adding layers of understanding and growth as you progress, while always revisiting the basics of gospel, community, and mission along the way. Vision "leaks," so you will continually be casting vision and reminding yourselves of what you are doing and why you are doing it and living this life together.

PHASE 1: FIRST 6–8 MONTHS—LAYING A GOSPEL FOUNDATION

You will need to introduce anyone and everyone who may be interested in living on mission with you to the vocabulary and theology that lay the foundation for making disciples and forming MCs. You are starting to call yourself, your family, and others to "die to self" in many areas of life, beginning a journey that will forever change you all. Growing together in your gospel fluency and helping those in your immediate family to be rightly motivated for a life on mission are the most critical aspects as you begin. There is really no way to put a perfect timeframe or absolute schedule to this phase; we will all continue to grow in light of the gospel for the rest of our lives!

Potential # of Weeks	Focus/Being	Activity/Doing
2–?	**Begin with your family and/or closest friends**	Sharing the things that you learned in Chapter 1 of this book with your spouse, kids and closest friends. Perhaps share this book and/or *Transformed* with others to stir up a desire for a life lived on mission together.
2–4	**Recruiting others for the adventure**	Sharing with your family the ideas and concepts found in Chapter 2. Praying for the Holy Spirit to prompt the hearts of a few others.
8–10	**Becoming an Incarnational Community** If you and your beginning group have a background of going to church and attending "small groups," you will want to start slowly and introduce the idea of incarnational living versus weekly attendance.	8-Week Tangible Kingdom Primer.* (Ask your group to make a strong 8-week commitment and decide where to go after this experience.)
	OR	
8–10	**Growing in the Gospel** If your initial "core team" is already convinced that life in a MC is for them, begin to go deeper into your understanding of the gospel in all of life. It is imperative that you start to form people in their true gospel-identity. Being leads to doing!	8-Week Gospel Primer.* Review Chapter 3 of this book.

2–4	**Who's In / Who's Out?** Not everyone who begins with you will want to continue. It is important not to lower the bar so as to try and convince everyone to stick around. Trust the Spirit!	Determine who will move forward as a family on mission. Based on your last 8 weeks or so together, who is ready to commit to a lifestyle of disciple-making as described in this book?
6–8	**What Next, Lord?** **Identifying the People of Peace in your lives** As a group begins to grow, have weekly "family dinner nights" together and work to increase the more organic overlap of your lives and schedules.	Review Chapters 4 and 5. Those who have committed should begin to pray for your People of Peace, asking the Spirit to show you "what's next" with each as you pray toward inviting them to participate in the Story-formed Way with you and your community. Be bold — trust God here!
(5–6 mo. point)		You may want to suggest reading the book *Leading Missional Communities*, as a community, over these same weeks. Spend an evening or two discussing Appendix B: The Discipleship Environment of Jesus.

My wife and I have had the opportunity and privilege to be a part of starting several missional communities (and new church plants) from scratch. The beginning months are always filled with the fear of, "What if no one else wants to do this? What if none of our friends or neighbors, those who are not-yet-believers, want to hang out and lean into the amazing good news of Jesus and his Kingdom with us?" But each time, as we have stepped out in faith, God has shown that he has gone before us to touch the hearts of his own, and those he is calling into the Family.

This is his work!

We have also learned that everything pivots and orbits initially around our own family. To the degree that we live on mission, treating everyone whom God brings around (or sends us to) like family, our community has grown, learned, and expanded to include the most unlikely of characters. Understanding the immensity of the good news of the gospel changes everything and paves the way for this type of life — the life that Jesus died to give us.

PHASE 2: NEXT 6 MONTHS — MATURING MISSIONAL COMMUNITIES

By now you should be moving toward understanding and fostering more mature rhythms in your MC, moving well beyond a weekly meeting and developing new daily rhythms and connections as a family of missionary servants. Both your organized activities and your organic interactions should be increasing. Life together is probably feeling more and more like a loving, caring family. Conversations and interactions that you are having should be increasingly gospel-centered:

discipling people to the truth, in very natural ways. Soon you will begin to form a community covenant (see Appendix C) that helps further articulate how you want to live your lives together on mission. It also helps identify who specifically you feel called, as a group, to make disciples of and among. You will notice at this point that there are some folks who are more committed to this mission than others, and (hopefully) you have rings of relationship going outward via POP (People of Peace). Not everyone is at the same place in this journey; that's okay! Continue to plan, lead, and share responsibility for the mission with those who are "leaning in" to relationship and mission.

Potential # of Weeks	Focus/Being	Activity/Doing
10–14	**Going Deeper as a Family—The Story** Now you begin to move your People of Peace past casual, organic relational activities. The "challenge" level goes up relationally as you begin to engage the Bible together in community. Your "risk" becomes an offer of life!	Begin to go through the Story-formed Way with your core community and those POP who have agreed to experience this with you in relationship.
2	**Seeding Multiplication into Everything** Just one or two people should not be leading, organizing, and doing everything in your MC. Remember to MAWL (page 142) people as they develop and grow.	Review with your MC the ideas and concepts found in Chapter 6. Make course corrections for anything you are presently doing as a community that is not reproducible.
4–6	**A Covenant Community** A covenant is a promise between people to live and be a certain way in relationship with one another. Creating a Community Covenant will help you solidify the organized aspects of your life together and identify a specific people and context in which you will continue to seek POP and those God has for you to disciple.	Prayerfully work through the Covenant Questionnaire found in Appendix C with those in the community who are committed to the mission and are stepping into leadership within the family. Also talk through the Missional Community Assessment Starter available for download at www.gcmcollective.org/article /contextualization-assessment-starter.

6–8	**Breathe In, Breathe Out** Depending on the season, and what the culture around you is involved in recreationally, you will naturally find that there are times of "breathing in," when your community focuses on gospel growth and discipleship; and there will be times when you focus on "breathing out" and establishing new relationships as you look for more POP.	Increase the frequency of eating at the same restaurants or visiting a local pub. Join a league or team of some sort. Make the kids' sports teams and their parents an increased focus of generosity and hospitality as you intentionally build new friendships.
(About 1-year point)		Discuss as a community ways to increase the organic interactions you have together, as a group or individually, throughout each week. Look for needs that you can meet in each other's lives as a reminder and demonstration of the gospel. Review Chapter 8 of this book.

There is nothing more formative in the communities that we have been a part of, and the hundreds of others that we have coached, than the times we have spent going through the Story-formed Way. Helping people understand the overarching narrative of God's gospel story from Genesis to Jesus is *always* life changing! As things start picking up speed, my tendency is to sit back a little, take it easy, and relish in our newfound "success." But I've learned to keep an eye on the reproducibility of everything we're doing from the beginning. Do you know how you can tell if what you're doing and teaching is reproducible? Others will be reproducing it. Simple, huh?

Another powerful discovery along the way has been the creation of a Community Covenant. The very process of going through each aspect of our gospel identity (family, missionary, servant, disciple) and how we will live this identity out in the normal rhythms of life (see Chapter 6) has proven to be a powerful aspect of our discipleship and has brought a laser-like focus to those whom specifically we are called to make disciples of.

PHASE 3: NEXT 6–8 MONTHS— MULTIPLYING LEADERS AND COMMUNITY

Celebrate the last year or so that you have been together by throwing a larger than usual party or going on a weekend retreat together!

Now that the foundation for discipleship and mission have been laid, it's time to move toward identifying, developing, and planning the release of leaders for future MCs. You will begin to plan for the multiplication of MCs throughout your city or region. At this point you should also have new(er) people in your extended family who weren't with you at the very beginning. They also need the basics of *gospel, community,* and *mission* laid out and passed on to them in reproducible ways.

It is a very common mistake to forget to "begin at the beginning" with new family members, making the assumption that they'll just catch up over time. Just as a new baby in the family must be taught the same basics in life that their older siblings now master, so too do our new brothers and sisters in the community need to learn the foundations of life on mission. At this point there are multiple layers of experiences, teachings, and discipleship going on. As with any healthy, growing family, there needs to be a constant re-starting for younger members and continued growth for maturing saints.

Potential # of Weeks	Focus/Being	Activity/Doing
4–8	**New Family Initiation** Introducing the concepts and learning that you, your family, and initial core members went through together. These times may happen all together or perhaps with just a few of the "older" brothers and sisters helping teach the "younger."	Teach/share with newer family members the things that you learned in this book and/or *Transformed*. Ask them to read these resources and get together to discuss the implications. You may consider taking a few weeks as a community to discuss the short but poignant book *Be the Church*, which is available for free download at www.vergenetwork.org /bethechurch/.
8–10	**(Re)Laying Gospel Foundations** Growing together in your gospel fluency and helping everyone to be rightly motivated by the gospel is crucial for everyone — especially those newer to the community. Don't fear repeating things: let those who are more gospel-fluent lead others, passing on and reproducing what God has taught them.	Depending on the background and familiarity to missional concepts of the newer people in your community, you will, as appropriate, want to take them through either the Gospel Primer or the Tangible Kingdom Primer.
Concurrent	**Identifying and Developing New Leaders** Concurrent to developing the new members of your MC in the basics, you will need to be identifying those leaders who will most likely be ready to be sent to multiply with others into a new missional family. Don't skip this important step, thinking that people aren't ready. Healthy things grow!	Review Chapter 7 of this book and ask the Holy Spirit to show you which people have demonstrated maturity in the 4 Cs in their life so far. Meet with these people to discuss this and call them to the next level of discipleship and maturity within your extended family.

10–14	**Making New Disciples and Developing New Leaders** Continuing to lay the foundations for new disciples, it is time to begin to ground them in the Story of God found in the Bible. This is a perfect opportunity for new leaders to pass on what they have received as they start to help lead the Story-formed Way. Don't cut new leaders loose on this; remember MAWL!	Begin to go through the Story-formed Way again for the sake of the new POP and newer members of the community who have yet to experience this. Those who have been through the SFW will go much deeper through the experience this time!
Concurrent	**Multiplying Leaders** You will now create a new rhythm within your MC: a leadership "huddle" and intentional equipping time each week. This is for those whom you have identified and who have "stepped up" to greater leadership in your MC. These times are a bit more formal and organized, helping this group of leaders to grow in their gospel fluency and their ability to find POP and lead others into a life as a family on mission.	Begin to meet as a circle of leaders, training and equipping in the areas that are most needed for continued growth and as preparation for their leading their own MCs in the near future. A helpful exercise and discovery process is to take your leaders through a 5-Fold Ministry (APEST) assessment. This helps identify a leader's natural giftedness within the framework of Ephesians 4. I suggest using this free survey: http://fivefoldsurvey.com/.

In the early years of living in community and sending others out to do the same, I think we often waited too long before releasing (or shoving) qualified people out to lead and multiply the mission. Given that we had people, often couples, who exhibited maturity in the 4 Cs of leadership, I realized over time that the best way for them to grow in *their* discipleship is for them to begin to lead others. Jesus is brilliant! He knew (and I'm finally learning it) that if we really want people to be more like Jesus, then we need to send them out to make disciples of Jesus.

Corresponding to the issue of equipping and sending new leaders, I've noticed the tendency to take my eye off the reality that the newer folks coming into the orb of life in our community need the foundational stuff that my current leaders received and experienced. You must always be laying gospel foundations and discipleship basics from the beginning *and* all the way up the leadership slope. Don't fear repeating the basics—often. Even strong leaders tend to need it.

PHASE 4: NEXT 6 MONTHS AND BEYOND— LAUNCHING KINGDOM MOVEMENTS

Now we begin to think, pray, and look toward creating a gospel movement that will change our city! What would it look like for multiple missional communities to now begin to gather together (re-congregate) for training and the sending of new MCs throughout your city or region? You may be tempted to think, "It's too soon to start new MCs from within our extended family." This is where training and trust come together. If you have prayerfully (led by the Spirit) followed the steps to identify and disciple those in your community, and you have spent time intentionally *training* your leaders to one day lead an extended family of their own, it is now time to *trust* that God has gone before you and will walk with those whom you send to continue on Jesus' mission of making disciples. This won't happen accidentally; it takes an increased level of intentionality and faith.

Potential # of Weeks	Focus/Being	Activity/Doing
4	**Preparing to Launch New Communities** Soon you will need to prayerfully decide who God seems to be leading to start a new missional community, one that will grow out of their own family on mission. Look for those who have enlarging visions for their own neighbors and POP in their life. Pray for faith, wisdom, and courage to follow the Spirit into a new season of mission and ministry!	Read through *Multiplying Missional Leaders* by Mike Breen in your leaders "huddle." Use this as a guide to determine the next areas of development that each of your leaders need and desire.
2	**Covenant Review** From time to time it is helpful to collectively take a look at the Community Covenant that you created together several months back. The leaders who are preparing to start new MCs should begin to work on what a covenant could look like for their new community, working on this with anyone who may be planning to join them. From my experience, this will be a time of great reflection, repentance, and development.	Use your Community Covenant as a diagnostic tool to determine which parts of life together in community on mission you have been faithful to carry out, and which areas you need to ask God to give you strength and obedience in.
4 – 8	**Dig in Deeper** It is quite possible that your discussion and prayer around your covenant has illuminated areas that your community needs to grow in together and individually.	Take the time as needed to study a particular part of the Bible or do a book study that will help you grow where needed.

6–8	**Breathe In, Breathe Out … Again** While focusing on new leaders who will soon be launching out, don't lose pace with the rest of the growing community. Continue to lead them out on mission, building new relationships and seeking their own People of Peace.	As a community grows in diversity, so do the opportunities to meet new people and make more disciples. Look for new rhythms of the culture around you that you can engage in as a community.
Between 12–18 months in, plan to multiply	**Out of the Nest** While it is impossible to predict an exact length of time it takes to equip someone to lead a missional community, I encourage you to "begin to begin," keep your leaders close to you, and see them often. But release them to start new communities within 12–18 months or so of beginning to live in a community on mission with you. God is greater than any fears or obstacles they have or perceive.	It is important to begin regular coaching with leaders and teams that have been sent to start new MCs. In essence, you are continuing your leadership "huddles" with the topics and equipping that are geared specifically to current needs and growth.
When you have multiple MCs in your city	**A Re-Gathered Community** A natural outflow of coming from the same healthy, growing family or tribe is that you want to see each other and you desire to be updated on what your other brothers and sisters are experiencing out on mission. Bringing these MCs together is a natural and historical way to see new "churches planted" in your city.	Monthly, bi-monthly, or weekly gatherings of multiple MCs are now a way to share resources, teaching, and worship gifts and stay connected as a growing extended family on mission to your city.

The path of least resistance continually calls us to just sort of chug along with those closest to us in our missional community and call it "good." Starting to think about rapid multiplication and larger, combined gatherings always sounds as overwhelming and as all-consuming as it did when we started our first MC. But look where God has taken you! Just as you took initial steps of faith into community at the beginning, now you must trust the Spirit for what lies ahead. Continue to practice the prayer, "What next, Lord?" for everyone in your community and for this blossoming movement in your city. Seek out others around you to go on the next leg of this journey—they're out there.

While all of this is certainly a journey, taken one step at a time, I want to call you to have a great sense of gospel urgency as you grow on God's mission. There is no other church or set of saints on this planet. It's us—you and I. This is our season and opportunity to fulfill the very purpose for which we've been created and saved. It's not that we *have* to, but we *get* to bring the greatest message about the greatest King who ever lived into all the world, starting with our little corner of it. I pray that the Good News will so grip your heart and life that everything else will begin to seem pale and weak and less valuable.

THE DISCIPLESHIP ENVIRONMENT OF JESUS

For Jesus, discipleship was never a curriculum or a series of events and classes that he asked his disciples to attend. Today, while such resources and experiences can teach you what Jesus taught, they don't create an experience where people learn to *obey* all that he commanded in every area of life. A gospel-centered community living together on Jesus' mission is the necessary context for biblical discipleship.

Life on life. Life in community. Life on mission.

Discipleship is an all-of-life apprenticeship led by Jesus himself. In order to make disciples of Jesus, who in turn know how to make more disciples, we must pay close attention to the *experience* and *environment* that Jesus provided his disciples. It is critical to keep in mind that *all* discipleship must be

- Spirit led

- Gospel saturated

- Community based

- Individually tailored

- Holistic

- Frequent and long-term

- Modeled and experienced

- Organized and organic

- Others focused

SPIRIT LED

Discipleship is the process of moving from unbelief to belief concerning what is true of God, and now us, in every area of life. It is the Holy Spirit who draws us to the Father, reminds us of the truth, and transforms us into God's family of missionary servants. The Spirit calls, equips, and sends us out to bear fruit for his glory, through his power.

The Holy Spirit is the primary discipler of people.

We will never make disciples apart from being in submission to and in partnership with the Holy Spirit.

Study these verses to learn more: Galatians 3:1–4; 5:16–26; John 14:15–20; 16:7–15; 1 Corinthians 2:10–14; Romans 8:5–14.

Ask yourself: What would it look like to disciple others with greater submission to and dependence on the Holy Spirit?

GOSPEL SATURATED

In the New Testament we often see Jesus lead the disciples to reflect and apply truth based on experience. In the course of everyday events and conversations, he showed them how being a part of his kingdom gives a new perspective on all of life, changing everything.

The gospel must permeate the discipling environment. It is the good news for *every* area of our life, not just good news about our afterlife. The gospel answers every problem, changes fear to faith, and gives us the motivation to submit all of life to the lordship of Jesus. In him alone we find our security, significance, approval, joy, and satisfaction.

Study these verses to learn more: Ephesians 4:15; Galatians 2:14; John 14:6; Hebrews 3:13; 2 Corinthians 4:13; 1 Thessalonians 5:11.

Ask yourself: Do casual conversations in community often go to the gospel? How can I help saturate the discipling environment with the gospel and help others grow in their gospel fluency as well?

COMMUNITY BASED

Jesus himself embodied all truth, yet he chose to call a very diverse group of people to live with and follow him in community. The disciples learned an extraordinary amount from watching and listening to Jesus, and then they talked about, questioned, and lived out what they learned together.

None of us are perfectly like Jesus on our own; it takes a Spirit-led community to represent him and function fully as his body. We need each other's various gifts, experiences, and perspectives to draw us into a deeper understanding of the gospel. Character qualities such as love, compassion, sacrifice, and generosity are more likely to be integrated into a person's life in the context of relationship.

Study these verses to learn more: Matthew 20:17–28; John 17:20–26; Luke 9:1–20; Ephesians 4:4–13; 1 Corinthians 14:26–33.

Ask yourself: Does everyone in my community see themselves as a vital component to everyone else's discipleship process?

INDIVIDUALLY TAILORED

Though we most often find Jesus spending time with the disciples in community, we also see him speaking specifically into the lives of individual followers at different times and in unique ways.

In addition to the need for a consistent and dynamic group environment, discipleship must have a personal nature as well. Each individual in our community has different needs, challenges, passions, and spiritual gifts. Their discipleship will require personalized attention in addition to the things they do and learn together.

In the same way that parents view the development of each of their children individually, discipleship must also focus on the unique needs of the person.

Study these verses to learn more: Matthew 14:28–31; 16:15–19; 26:36–38; Luke 9:28; 22:31–34; 2 Timothy 1:13; 3:10–17.

Ask yourself: Is someone giving regular and personal care to each member of my community based on their needs and personality?

HOLISTIC

It's obvious from the teaching and experiences Jesus had with the disciples that he was committed to developing them holistically. He desired to bring every area of their lives under his kingdom rule and reign.

Discipleship involves caring for the whole life of a person. Every part of our life needs the gospel, not just the "spiritual" things such as Bible study, prayer, and sin issues. How we steward our time, jobs, money, relationships, entertainment, and health and body must all be transformed by the gospel for God's glory.

Study these verses to learn more: Matthew 5:1–12; 6:1–4, 19–34; Luke 5:5–11; 6:37–42.

Ask yourself: What areas of discipleship and "all of life" care do I need to give greater attention to in our missional community? How can we begin to disciple one another more holistically?

FREQUENT AND LONG-TERM

Jesus invested three years of his life into his disciples before he sent them to minister and lead on their own. During that time he spent an incredible amount of time with them—often with all twelve, sometimes with a few, occasionally one-to-one. Life together with Jesus was not just a weekly meeting.

Discipleship is not fast; it takes a lot of time, commitment, and sacrificial love for one another. We must be with those we are discipling frequently and expect to walk with them for a long period of time. We would never imagine that we could parent our children in a couple of hours each week and expect them to be healthy and mature adults. Discipleship is much the same.

Study these verses to learn more: Matthew 4:18–23; 9:35–38; Mark 3:14; 10:32; Luke 8:1; John 6:60–71.

Ask yourself: Are we spending enough time together, seeing and experiencing life as a community, to the point that true life change can happen?

MODELED AND EXPERIENCED

Most of the time Jesus spent with his disciples was in the normal rhythms of life as they ate, traveled, taught, and served others. While there were times when Jesus taught in more formal settings, it was his consistent example of love, generosity, encouragement, and prayer that probably had the greatest impact on their lives.

Jesus modeled the life he wanted his disciples to go and live.

We all learn much more when we see something modeled and then experience it for ourselves compared with just hearing it taught. Disciples need to *see* and *experience* a gospel-centered life modeled for them in the day-to-day lives of mature saints.

Study these verses to learn more: Matthew 8; 9:9–13; 14:13–21; Luke 5:12–13; 8:25–56; 13:10–17; 14:1–6; 17:11–14.

Ask yourself: Do those in my community have access to every area of my life so they can see and experience the gospel at work? How can we encourage others in the community to live out more of what they see modeled in our lives?

ORGANIZED AND ORGANIC

Jesus often spent times teaching at the temple and synagogues, and he regularly participated in annual feasts and traditions. But he also trained his followers in the moments that occurred along the road, at a casual meal, or in chance conversations that would come up in life. The discipleship model of Jesus included both *organized* activities and *organic* opportunities.

Just as our natural, healthy family life contains both of these elements, we will need to nurture our extended families in the organized and organic parts of life in community. Healthy community life will include planned-out events and reoccurring activity, but it is also filled with spontaneous and unplanned opportunities throughout each week.

If your missional community is only doing organized things—event to event—it will grow stale and be unfulfilling. If your group is only interested in the organic, unplanned "hanging out" together, it will rarely be on mission or make mature disciples.

Study these verses to learn more: Matthew 5:1–12; Mark 14:12–18, 22; Luke 10:25–28, 38–42; 12:1–11; 14:1–4; 21:37.

Ask yourself: Which do I most naturally prefer: organized events or organic interactions? How can I begin to grow in both these practices?

OTHERS FOCUSED

Jesus placed a high value on service and evangelism to those who were not yet his followers, especially to those in great need. Jesus was consistently exposing the disciples to different kinds of people, in different kinds of places, with different kinds of needs. He often placed the disciples in situations where they could learn to love and serve "the least of these" by serving alongside him.

Spiritual growth is often more significant when we serve others outside our own close circle and those who are in great need. It's very important for these things to be practiced frequently so that they become part of a person's lifestyle rather than a project that they participate in on occasion.

Study these verses to learn more: Matthew 8:1–3, 14–17; 10:5–8; Luke 9:10–17; 18:35–43.

Ask yourself: How can I make mission-minded service a larger part of my missional community's life together? What can I begin to do weekly or monthly as a service to those in need around me?

[Note: I want to gratefully acknowledge my brother and partner in the gospel, Todd Morr, for his original thoughts and outline on the environment that Jesus made disciples in. His fingerprints are all over and throughout this resource.]

RESOURCE TOOLBOX

Here are a few resources that I either have mentioned along the way or want to point you toward on your journey:

ONLINE

10-Week Story-formed Way Experience This is a set of narratives and dialog that help form people in the gospel and their understanding of the big picture of the Bible, http://www.gcmcollective.org/article/story-formed-way

Story Training Videos In these videos you will receive training to prepare you to tell the Story and lead the dialog in an effective way. http://www.gcmcollective.org/story-training

Be the Church: Discipleship and Mission Made Simple This short but powerful free eBook will help introduce people to the basics of life on mission. http://www.vergenetwork.org/bethechurch

Contextualization Assessment Starter This worksheet will help your community to better understand the people and context to which you have been sent to make disciples. http://www.gcmcollective.org/article/contextualization-assessment-starter

Covenant Questionnaire This tool will help you create a Missional Community Covenant, helping you to identify very specifically many aspects of your shared life on mission in community. http://caesarkalinowski.com/covenant

APEST Survey A helpful exercise and discovery process to take your leaders through a fivefold ministry (APEST) assessment. http://fivefoldsurvey.com

3DM Launch This is a two-year learning community that can offer you the very best training and coaching for starting and multiplying missional communities and planting churches. http://launch.3dmovements.com

Twitter Follow the author: @CaesarKal

WEBSITES

http://caesarkalinowski.com

http://www.gcmcollective.org

http://www.vergenetwork.org

http://wearesoma.com/resources/

http://3dmovements.com

BOOKS

Transformed — A New Way of Being Christian
Caesar Kalinowski

The Tangible Kingdom
Hugh Halter and Matt Smay

Leading Missional Communities
Mike Breen

Family on Mission
Mike Breen

The Gospel Primer
Caesar Kalinowski, http://missiopublishing.com

The Tangible Kingdom Primer
Hugh Halter and Matt Smay, http://missiopublishing.com

Everyday Church: Gospel Communities on Mission
Tim Chester and Steve Timmis

NOTES

Chapter 1: Looking Back to Move Forward

1. I prefer the term "not-yet believer" to "lost person." I find it so much more hopeful and respectful, and the New Testament never once refers to anyone as being a "lost person."
2. Hugh Halter and Matt Smay, *AND: The Gathered and Scattered Church*, Exponential Series (Grand Rapids: Zondervan, 2010), 52. Kindle edition.
3. Zechariah 4:10 KJV.
4. Luke 13:18.
5. Luke 13:20.
6. Matthew 13:44–46.
7. John 21:4–6.
8. This is a great story of how God called and led us into this journey; you can read more about it in my book *Transformed*.
9. John 5:19–22.
10. Luke 6:29 paraphrased.
11. Matthew 20:26–28 paraphrased.
12. See Matthew 25:34–40.
13. See Mark 11:23.

Chapter 2: Me, Myself, and Mine

1. Take a look for yourself: http://allrecipes.com/recipe/broccoli -chicken-divan/.
2. Luke 9:57–62.
3. Luke 9:59.
4. Luke 9:61.
5. I have received much insight and understanding regarding these three types of potential disciples of Jesus from the writings of author William MacDonald in his poignant book *True Discipleship* (Ontario, Canada: Gospel Folio Press, 2003).

6. Luke 14:26.
7. Luke 14:33.
8. Dietrich Bonhoeffer, *The Cost of Discipleship* (London: SCM Press, 1948/2001), 44.
9. C. S. Lewis, *Mere Christianity* (New York: Collier Books, 1960), 167.
10. Luke 14:28–30.
11. Steve Timmis is a friend and author and one of the founding leaders of Crowded House in Sheffield, England. He lives and leads others in gospel-centered communities. Check out his books.

Chapter 3: Gospel Motivation

1. See my book *Transformed*, especially the first two chapters, for a thorough look at our new identity in Christ.
2. Genesis 1:26 paraphrased. See also verses 27–28.
3. Genesis 1:31.
4. I have had some eye-opening help on these thoughts regarding reintroducing the entire story—the bigger picture—from a few comments I heard author Rob Bell make several years ago in a lecture, and more recently from a talk given by Andy Crouch at a Q Conference. Thank you, brothers. See http://www.qideas.org/video/power.aspx.
5. Hugh Halter, *Flesh: Bringing the Incarnation Down to Earth* (Colorado Springs: David C. Cook, 2014), 54.
6. See my book *Transformed* for a fuller understanding of this.
7. Matthew 28:19.
8. Tim Chester, *A Meal with Jesus: Discovering Grace, Community, and Mission around the Table* (Wheaton, IL: Crossway, 2011), 45. Kindle edition.
9. John 16:8.

Chapter 4: Saints and Sinners

1. Hugh Halter, *Flesh: Bringing the Incarnation Down to Earth* (Colorado Springs: David C. Cook, 2014), 6.
2. Tim Chester, *A Meal with Jesus: Discovering Grace, Community, and Mission around the Table* (Wheaton, IL: Crossway, 2011). Kindle edition.
3. Matthew 11:19.
4. Luke 7:37–38.

5. Chester, *A Meal with Jesus,* 39. Kindle edition.

6. John 15:11–15 MSG.

7. John 8:31–32.

8. Romans 5:8.

9. 1 John 4:19; Matthew 5:43–48.

10. Mark 10:45 ESV, emphasis added.

11. Luke 19:10.

12. Luke 7:34.

13. Luke 5:27–39.

14. Luke 7:36–50.

15. Luke 9:10–17.

16. Luke 10:38–42.

17. Luke 11:37–54.

18. Luke 14.

19. Luke 19:1–10.

20. Luke 22:7–21.

21. Luke 24:13–16, 28–35. My insights on all these meals come from a great study and observation done by Tim Chester in *A Meal with Jesus.*

22. Luke 10:1–9 NLT.

23. http://bensternke.com/2010/11/zacchaeus-as-a-person-of-peace/. I want to acknowledge all the learning I have gleaned regarding People of Peace from my friends at 3DM, including Mike and Sally Breen, Jo Saxton, Dave Rhodes, and Ben Sternke.

24. Luke 15:3–6.

25. To grow in gospel fluency in community, I recommend this eight-week experience: The Gospel Primer. http://www.missiopublishing.com /the-gospel-primer.

26. Ben Sternke. http://bensternke.com/2010/11/zacchaeus-as-a-person -of-peace.

Chapter 5: Into the Fray

1.   Mike Breen, *Leading Missional Communities* (Pawleys Island, SC: 3DM, 2013), 7. Kindle edition.

2. Ibid.

3. Luke 10:16.

4. Breen, *Leading Missional Communities,* 25–26.

5. See John 8:31–32.

6. More about that in Chapter 7; also see Resource Toolbox in Appendix C.

7. *Transformed*, 98. I have shared this story and example many times and have always found it to be both encouraging and super practical. This process of "What next, Lord?" is really the beginnings of a life lived in and directed by the Holy Spirit.

8. Breen, *Leading Missional Communities*, 28.

9. These beloved pink platters have been in our family longer than I've been alive. I ate every holiday and birthday meal in my family on them when I was growing up. Now I have them, and Team K continues to enjoy our special meals on these indestructible plates. http://ow.ly/s1LBz.

10. Breen, *Leading Missional Communities*, 30.

11. Ibid.

12. http://swaggle.mobi/

13. DNA stands for Discipleship, Nurture, and Accountability. I got this simple acronym and pattern from Michael Frost. We form three-person DNA groups (men with men, women with women) and disciple one another's hearts on a weekly basis. This is similar to the Huddles that 3DM teaches about where deeper heart and gospel issues are addressed in smaller communities within the broader community.

14. I came across this important understanding (proactive and reactive mission) while having a conversation sitting on the beach with my brilliant friend and author Tim Chester.

Chapter 6: The Seed Principle

1. For our family recipe go to http://caesarkalinowski.com/salamieggs.

2. Mark 8:1–21.

3. Mark 8:17–21 NLT.

4. Genesis 1:28.

5. Genesis 9:7.

6. Genesis 35:11 ESV.

7. Matthew 28:18–20.

8. Habakkuk 2:14.

9. See Hebrews 1:3.

10. 2 Corinthians 3:18 NIV (1984 ed.).

11. Psalm 72:19.

12. More on this from Hugh and Matt can be found in their very helpful book *The Tangible Kingdom* and in a tool for working this out in your community, *The Tangible Kingdom Primer*. Both are available at http://www.missiopublishing.com.

13. This is a basic principle that many have used over the years to help disciples balance their lives. I have learned much on using this tool from Mike Breen and the 3DM team.

14. *Transformed* and *The Gospel Primer* can help you grow immensely in this area.

15. See the Toolbox in Appendix C for more information on the Story-formed Way.

16. Breen, *Leading Missional Communities,* 10.

17. You may need to start here with something like *The Tangible Kingdom Primer* or *The Gospel Primer* or the Story-formed Way. These are all resources that you can use together in community over several weeks. It may help to use one of these tools to break old patterns and under-standings and/or introduce and grow in new understanding. Check out Appendix C for a sample Community Covenant and a template for creating one in your community.

Chapter 7: Yeast in the Dough

1. Matthew 13:24–30 NLT.

2. Matthew 13:33 NLT.

3. Mark 10:21.

4. The story of my experience in Soma and our practice as a community is told at length in *Transformed.*

5. 2 Timothy 2:2.

6. Mike Breen (2012–05–10), *Multiplying Missional Leaders.* Kindle edition (Kindle Locations 1447–1455).

7. See 1 Corinthians 5:6.

8. John 5:19 paraphrased.

9. Mark 4:26–29.

10. John 12:24.

Chapter 9: Sometimes Sunday Happens

1. 1 Corinthians 14:26–33 MSG, emphasis added.
2. Frank Viola and George Barna (2008-01-17). *Pagan Christianity? Exploring the Roots of Our Church Practices* (Carol Stream, IL: Barna-Books, 2008), 77. Kindle edition.
3. Leviticus 23.
4. Exodus 12; Leviticus 23.
5. 1 Corinthians 11:23–26.
6. Matthew 15:1–3.
7. Michael Frost and Alan Hirsch, *The Shaping of Things to Come* (Peabody, MA: Hendrickson Publishers, LLC, 2003), 68.
8. Hebrews 10:24–25 KJV.
9. See Ephesians 4:7–13.
10. See John 17:21–23.

Conclusion: A Kingdom Movement

1. G. K. Chesterton, *What's Wrong with the World* (1910), end of chapter 14 in part 4.